Till

Justice

is

Done

Till Justice is Done

by Diana Eiranova-Kyle

Book design by Charles King.

This is a narrative based on court records, media accounts, and the personal experiences of the members of the Coalition for Justice. The dialogue recounted in this book, while not verbatim, reflects the substance of what was said to the best of the author's recollection and/or that of others present.

ISBN-13: 978-1484074213
ISBN-10: 1484074211

ACKNOWLEDGEMENTS

To my beloved Charlie . . . You are the wind beneath my wings.

To Meca Sorrentini and Dolores Huerta, my two "Pacha Mamas," who mentored me and nurtured my passion for social justice, and who will continue to inspire me for the rest of my life.

To the members of the Coalition for Justice and to the many friends who inspired me to write this book, for playing an invaluable role in helping justice be done.

To my brilliant and caring editor and mentor, Sister Jean Hughes, O.P.

And to Charles King, who designed the first and last edition of *Till Justice is Done* with selfless care and generosity.

FOREWORD

This is the story of the Coalition for Justice, a group of Latino and religious advocates who came together to promote the innocence of two men they believed had been erroneously and repeatedly convicted of a terrible crime.

In February of 1983, Jeanine Nicarico, a ten-year-old from the western suburbs of Chicago, was abducted from her home, raped, and murdered. A year later, Rolando Cruz, Alejandro "Alex" Hernandez and Stephen Buckley were indicted despite the lack of physical evidence against them. In February of 1985, jurors deadlocked on Buckley and sentenced the two Latinos to death. Months later, while confessing to two unrelated murders, a convicted sex offender by the name of Brian Dugan acknowledged killing Jeanine Nicarico.

Notwithstanding Dugan's confession, Cruz and Hernandez spent more than ten years in prison before being released in November of 1995. As for Dugan, while his DNA closely matches the genetic material found at the crime scene, to this day he has not been charged.

ABOUT THE AUTHOR

After working as a journalist and community activist, Diana Eiranova-Kyle founded a volunteer organization of Latino and Interfaith leaders which successfully advocated for the exoneration of the two wrongfully convicted men who are the focus of this book. Ms. Eiranova-Kyle wrote *Till Justice is Done* upon graduating from Columbia College in 2000 with a Masters in Journalism. As stated on the book's back cover by her friend and mentor Dolores Huerta, "*Till Justice is Done* not only documents the Coalition for Justice's successful efforts to promote the innocence of Alejandro Hernandez and Rolando Cruz but will undoubtedly inspire others to take a stand against injustice." In addition to endorsing this book, Dolores Huerta got Ms. Eiranova-Kyle a grant to write and produce a 16 minute documentary film of the same name. "Till Justice is Done" premiered at an event where more than 250 people gathered to honor law enforcement individuals who lost their careers due to the wrongful prosecution of Rolando Cruz and Alex Hernandez. In 2006, Ms. Eiranova-Kyle wrote her first feature film script, "The Last Confession," based on her husband's life in the priesthood and on her research of the Roman Catholic Church's internal politics and business practices. "The Last Confession" won 3rd place in the 2009 Vision Fest Feature Screenwriting Competition in New York. Currently, Ms. Eiranova-Kyle is putting the finishing touches on a second screenwriting project, "DNA," which brings back the main characters from "The Last Confession" to help exonerate a man wrongfully accused of murder.

Contents

The Awakening

IT HAD BEEN A LONG DAY. After a two-hour ride from Stateville Correctional Center, I looked forward to a relaxing evening at home. I had gone to the maximum security prison near Joliet to visit Juan Rivera, a young Puerto Rican who in 1993 had been convicted of raping and killing a babysitter from Waukegan. After discussing his case with renowned attorneys like Patrick Tuite, who had represented Juan at his second trial, I was convinced that the 29-year old was completely innocent of the charges that had landed him behind bars for the rest of his life.

Although the babysitter, Holly Staker, had been stabbed 27 times, no shred of physical evidence linked Juan to the crime, including the genetic material found in the girl's body. Still, the case against him had been painstakingly mounted on a purported confession Juan had signed after hours of uninterrupted police interrogation.

Troubled by the idea that despite the lack of evidence, Juan had been convicted not once, but twice, I grabbed a glass of iced tea and turned to the evening news. Clicking through the channels, a habit I had picked up while working as a reporter, I switched back and forth between the Spanish and the English versions avidly looking for an interesting sound bite that would take my mind off Juan's case.

"If it was up to me, we'd take these three guys into the basement and shoot them," said a voice. To my surprise, the remarks did not come from some cowboy in an old Western movie but from a DuPage County board member being interviewed in reaction to a settlement the county had agreed to pay that same day. According to the report, the $3.5 million settlement would be distributed among Rolando Cruz, Alejandro Hernandez, and Stephen Buckley, who had been wrongfully imprisoned fifteen years earlier for the rape and murder of Jeanine Nicarico.

I could not believe my ears. "How could a public official make such an inflammatory statement against these men, even after they had been legally exonerated?" While waiting for a reporter to ask the same question, the answer came to me. As long as the DuPage criminal justice system refused to indict Brian Dugan, the real murderer of Jeanine Nicarico, Cruz, Hernandez and Buckley would continue to be the subject of unscrupulous remarks. Unless somebody set the record straight once and for all...

CHAPTER I

The Coalition for Justice

"Coming together is a beginning; keeping together is progress; working together is success."

—Henry Ford.

IT WAS ONE OF THOSE UNPREDICTABLE Chicago days in late August 1991. Tito Vargas, the executive director of the Westtown Coalition, had called earlier to suggest we gather at *El Ñandú* for a relaxing evening among friends. "Tonight is *peña* night," he said referring to the South American version of a jam session that every Thursday filled the small Argentinean restaurant. "I'm meeting Carlos Arango for dinner. Thought you would like to join us."

When I arrived shortly before eight, both were already savoring *empanadas* and sipping Chilean wine. "You look tired," Tito said as he ushered me to a chair.

Carlos agreed. "Yeah, I think you're overdoing it. Look at me, always fresh as a daisy." Nodding, I wondered if my old friend had looked in the mirror lately. Managing a community agency in the Mexican *barrio* known as Pilsen had its perks, but rest and relaxation were not among them. As for myself, though, Carlos was right. Besides coordinating a blindness prevention program for Lions Clubs International, most evenings I left work and drove straight to state Senator Miguel del Valle's office to help him prepare for what promised to be the most challenging political battle of his life.

"Do you remember how we met for the first time?" Carlos loved to test my memory, especially if he thought it was rusty.

"It was at a demonstration for immigrants' rights in front of the Federal Building in 1984. I covered the event for *La Raza*," I said, alluding to the Spanish-language newspaper I had worked for between 1983 and 1985.

"My question was too easy," he complained with a grin. "After all, we spend half of our lives at demonstrations."

"Yeah, and the other half writing proposals," added Tito raising his glass for a toast. "To our health! At this rate, we'll need it."

I had begun hunting for the waiter's attention when I noticed Rita Bustos approaching our table with another woman. The energetic owner of *El Ñandú* loved to promote her restaurant as a place where political strategists and community organizers could mix business with pleasure. "These are the friends I told you about," Rita began without beating around the bush. "Guys, this is Lisa. She works as an English-Spanish interpreter at the DuPage County courthouse. I'm sure you won't mind if she joins you to tell you about an injustice involving two Latinos from Aurora."

Rita's "no nonsense" approach seemed to make Lisa a bit uncomfortable. She hesitated for a few seconds before accepting Carlos' invitation to sit at our table. "Don't worry," I said, trying to sound reassuring, "you're not interrupting anything."

As she spoke, though, I realized that Lisa's uneasiness had more to do with what she had witnessed that day than with our hostess' style. "I was at the sentencing hearing of Alejandro [Alex] Hernandez, a young Puerto Rican from Aurora convicted of killing 10-year old Jeanine Nicarico," she said slowly. "I still can't believe the judge gave Alex 80 years and refused to hear the pleas of three law enforcement officials willing to testify that another man is solely responsible for this terrible crime."

"Wait a minute," I interrupted. "Are you telling us that these guys would have cleared Hernandez and that the judge ignored them? Were these people qualified to discuss the case?" I asked.

"The answer to both questions is 'Yes.' One of them, Jeremy Margolis, was the Illinois State police director who supervised an independent scrutiny of the case. The other one, James Teal, was Naperville's chief of police at the time of the crime." According to Lisa, the day's event was just one more sad chapter in a convoluted legal saga that had started six years earlier when Alex and another Latino, Rolando Cruz, had become the main suspects in the kidnapping, rape and murder of the 10-year-old.

Back in February 1983, went on Lisa, the heads of the local police department and the DuPage County sheriff's office set up a task force after the girl's body was found in the Illinois Prairie Path, in the west suburban town of Naperville. Assuming that the crime had been committed to cover up a failed burglary attempt, investigators focused their probe on the largely Hispanic populated neighborhoods in and around eastern Aurora, which clung to Naperville like a poor cousin to a rich relative. "Thinking that the little girl had been killed because she was in the house at the time of the robbery," concluded Lisa, "they [the investigators] dismissed other possibilities and focused on the two Latinos."

"But how did Cruz and Hernandez get messed up in this?" interrupted Tito.

"Tips flooded the DuPage sheriff's office after a $10,000 reward was set just weeks after the murder," continued Lisa. "Eager to collect the money, Cruz and Hernandez, both of Aurora, became police informants, claiming to know details about the murder they said they had heard about in the streets. But the lies they told investigators, far from making them richer, ended up costing them their freedom."

"Wasn't there another man, a white guy, also charged with the murder?" I asked, vaguely remembering the case.

"Yes, his name was Stephen Buckley. The jurors who convicted Cruz and Hernandez couldn't reach a verdict on him so he got a mistrial and was later released." According to Lisa, aware that Buckley owned boots similar to the type that had left a print on the kicked-in door of the Nicarico's house, DuPage deputies had asked him to submit his shoes for comparison. Later, using the boots as evidence against him, Buckley had been charged with the crime. Luckily for Buckley, noted Lisa, his defense attorney had successfully challenged the prosecution's expert witness and jurors had been unable to reach a verdict.

Cruz and Hernandez, on the other hand, who according to Lisa had been implicated in the murder by their own flights of fancy and by a parade of questionable witnesses, were sentenced to death.

"But how could they even indict them on such flimsy evidence?" asked Tito.

"At the time, the race for state's attorney in DuPage County was a close call between the incumbent, J. Michael Fitzsimmons, and a second-time challenger, James Ryan," explained Lisa. "Fitzsimmons, more than likely in a desperate attempt to save his post, announced the indictments two weeks before the 1984 March primary and vowed to seek the death penalty against Cruz, Hernandez and Buckley on the eve of the election. As for Jim Ryan," continued Lisa, "after winning office, he followed in his predecessor's footsteps and secured the convictions – and death sentences – for Cruz and Hernandez, leaving Buckley in jail for about two years before finally releasing him."

"Political expediency," blurted Tito. "Ryan must have thought he had the right guys and didn't give it a second thought."

"Political expediency with a dose of racism," added Carlos. "Notice the guy he let go was white."

"And Buckley isn't the only white guy Jim Ryan let go," added Lisa speaking over the music as the *peña* was now in full force. "In 1985, a man by the name of Brian Dugan was arrested and charged with the rape and murder of two other victims. While confessing to the killings of those victims, Donna Schnorr, a nurse from Aurora, and Melissa Ackerman, a 7-year-old from Somonauk in neighboring LaSalle County, Dugan also acknowledged participating in Jeanine Nicarico's murder."

Carlos interrupted with an obvious question: "Didn't DuPage investigate this guy?"

I detected a surge of excitement in Lisa's voice. "They did but they never charged him," she paused. "But I don't want to get ahead of myself. A year before Dugan confessed to the Nicarico murder, a DuPage County detective involved in the investigation told his superiors that he was convinced Cruz and Hernandez were the wrong guys," added Lisa, noting that the detective, John Sam, had later resigned and even volunteered to testify for the defense.

"Are you telling us that this detective, John Sam, warned his superiors they were on the wrong track and that the state's attorney still went ahead with the indictments?" I asked in disbelief. "Who was in charge then, Fitzsimmons or Ryan?"

"The first trial started after Jim Ryan was sworn in as DuPage State's attorney, so I would have to say, Ryan was," pondered Lisa. "However, I'm not sure if he was already in office when Sam warned his superiors in the sheriff's office. Regardless, it was definitely Jim Ryan who oversaw the prosecution of Buckley, Cruz and Hernandez in 1985," she pointed out.

"So Ryan must have thought that despite Dugan's confession, at least Cruz and Hernandez had something to do with the Nicarico crime, right?" ventured Carlos.

"Well, yes. But all that changed after [Illinois State Police] Commander [Edward] Cisowski told Jim Ryan that he was convinced that Dugan alone had killed Jeanine Nicarico." According to Lisa, the DuPage State's attorney had personally asked Cisowski to investigate Dugan's claims. "Strangely enough," added Lisa as if she had unearthed a hidden truth," not only did Jim Ryan dismiss Cisowski's conclusion but asked the [Illinois] attorney general's office to investigate his handling of the probe."

"Are you telling us that after Cisowski confirmed that someone else had committed the crime, instead of reopening the investigation, Jim Ryan kept on pushing the prosecutions of Cruz and Hernandez?" asked an incredulous Tito.

"That's right," said Lisa, who added that Alex and Rolando had been convicted mostly due to the testimonies of jailhouse snitches and other witnesses who claimed they had spoken about their involvement.

"But wasn't there anything else?" I prodded.

"There were also shoe prints under the Nicarico window that prosecutors suggested had been left by either Cruz, Hernandez or both," said Lisa. "Oh, and according to them Rolando also made a 'vision' statement of the crime to two DuPage deputy sheriffs."

"Was any of this true?" I asked, almost anticipating the answer to my question.

"I don't think so," replied Lisa. As the cases against both men unfolded, she explained, defense attorneys had discovered that the shoe prints in question belonged to a size 6 girl's shoe. "As for the so called witnesses who knew of their involvement, many wanted to and some did recant their testimonies."

"And what about the 'vision' statement?" pressed Tito.

According to Lisa, the alleged statement, which DuPage considered the most damning piece of evidence against Cruz, had never been recorded, reported or heard of until days before his trial."

"What's going on? You all look like you need some cheering up," interrupted Manuel Guillot approaching our table. Manuel, Sen. del Valle's legislative aide, had agreed to join us as soon as he was done in the office. "Sorry I'm late," he whispered looking at his watch.

"This is Lisa. She's been telling us about two Latinos who were screwed by the system," said Carlos, whose ability to summarize complex issues was legendary.

"Actually, she's been telling us about a criminal case in DuPage County, where in 1983, a 10-year-old girl was found raped and murdered," explained Tito, whose own daughter was about Jeanine's age at the time of her death. "Apparently, the two, Rolando Cruz and Alex Hernandez, got mixed up in this terrible crime because they were trying to collect a reward. So, in 1984, they were indicted with another guy by the name of Stephen Buckley."

"In February of 1985, while Buckley's trial ended in a hung jury," resumed Lisa, "Rolando and Alex were convicted and sentenced to die. Three years later, the Illinois Supreme Court granted both Latinos new trials arguing they shouldn't have been tried together. In 1990, Cruz was convicted again and was given the death penalty. As for Alex, after getting a hung jury at a second trial, in May he was found guilty and today got sentenced to 80 years in prison," she concluded.

"We know there are people in prison who are innocent," editorialized Carlos," like the four Mexicans who were pardoned by the governor after doing ten years. I'm talking about the guys Margo de Ley and her organization helped set free. But this case seems worse than any other I've ever heard about," he noted. "Especially because of the people in law enforcement who claim Cruz and Hernandez are innocent."

Moved by Carlos' remarks, I sat quietly listening to the waning sounds of the *peña* and sipping the last glass of wine, my mind briefly wandering to my native Argentina, where thousands of political prisoners had lingered hopelessly in cells for years on end. Until that night, I had thought that in a country where people were presumed innocent until proven guilty, it was evidence, and only hard evidence, which convicted the guilty. This case would radically change my mind.

"By the way, what happened with Buckley?" asked Tito.

"Remember? Buckley was indicted because prosecutors claimed one of his boots had left the imprint found on the

Nicarico's entrance door," Lisa reminded us. "So after he got a mistrial and the prosecution's expert witness got sick, he remained in jail until Jim Ryan dropped the charges against him in March of 1987. By the way, here too, someone in law enforcement lost his job," she pointed out. According to Lisa, Phil Gilman, then director of the DuPage County Crime Lab, had resigned from his post after county investigators removed Buckley's boots from his lab before he could write a report that would have weakened their case. "Aware that Gilman's conclusions would not support their theory against Buckley, DuPage prosecutors hired a self-proclaimed expert who would. Fortunately for Buckley, his attorney did a good job at discrediting the so-called expert and while they were considering trying him again, the witness got sick and resigned from the case."

"So why didn't DuPage retry him, like they did with Cruz and Hernandez?" asked Manuel.

"I guess they probably couldn't find another expert witness who would testify to their liking," reflected Lisa, stressing the fact that for about two years, between February, 1985 and March, 1987, Buckley had remained in a DuPage cell. "Even after an FBI expert in 1986 confirmed Gilman's conclusion that Buckley's boot could not have made the print," she noted.

"But as we already know, Cruz and Hernandez weren't so lucky, right Lisa?" said Carlos sarcastically.

"Right. As I said before, while Alex' second trial also ended in a hung jury, he was tried a third time and today was sentenced to 80 years in prison. As for Rolando, he was convicted at his second trial and his death sentence is being appealed before the Illinois Supreme Court," she concluded.

It was getting late. Before leaving, though, I promised Lisa we would look into the case and thanked her for bringing it up to our attention.

The following day, I decided to poll my sources in the Spanish-language media. The first person I called was the editor of *La Raza*, Vicente Fentanes. While waiting on the phone, I remembered that after I had left in 1985, the offices of *La Raza* had been moved and a lot of the files had been lost. However, they should have something about the appeals and the second trials, I thought while still on hold.

"*Hola*, Diana. What's going on with Miguel?" asked Vicente, assuming I was calling about Del Valle and the possibility that, following a redistricting move, he would end up facing his colleague, Ted Lechowicz.

"We still don't know, but I'm calling you about Cruz and Hernandez," I replied.

"Funny that you should call," he noted. "I just did a feature story on the case. I even went to Menard Prison to interview Rolando Cruz. Why is Del Valle interested?"

"He's not. At least, not yet," I said.

Suddenly, our voices became relaxed, unguarded. We were no longer the senator's press secretary and the reporter fishing for an exclusive, but two colleagues discussing a puzzling murder case that, according to Vicente, had gone very much unnoticed in the Latino community. "Many people still think that if they keep their noses clean they won't be victimized by the criminal justice system. They don't believe that what happened to these guys could happen to them," he noted, suggesting that our involvement in the case could help change that misconception. "Come by tomorrow and I'll give you what I have," he offered.

"Here's my article, plus copies of court papers and the names and phone numbers of relatives and attorneys," said Vicente the following day handing me a bulky package.

"We need to set up a meeting with a few other people," I urged Carlos and Tito after reviewing the contents of the package.

"Let's meet in my office," proposed Tito.

Less than a month after our fortuitous encounter with Lisa at *El Ñandú*, Carlos, Tito and I met again at the Westtown Coalition, in Chicago's northwest side, to discuss the scope of our involvement in pursuing justice for the two Latinos. Joining us this time was Margo de Ley, the Midwest representative of *Hermandad Mexicana Nacional,* the organization that had helped clear the names of the four Mexicans Carlos had mentioned at *El Ñandú.* Sitting to Margo's right was Sister Jean Hughes, an Adrian Dominican from a coalition of Catholic religious communities known as the "8th Day Center for Justice," who besides her refreshing sense of humor, brought a 35-year commitment to peace and justice to the table.

Right across from Jean was Hector Diaz who, as the director of community affairs for the Commonwealth in Chicago, was responsible for the well being of the thousands of Puerto Ricans living in the Midwest, including

Alex Hernandez and his family. Sitting next to Hector was America "Meca" Sorrentini, a tireless promoter of the Puerto Rican cultural heritage and an equally tireless supporter of the emancipation of the island she called home. Right across from Meca was another Puerto Rican by the name of Pablo Medina. An outstanding mediator with the City of Chicago's Department of Human Relations, Pablo had a penchant for social issues. Sitting to Pablo's right was Bob Medina, also Puerto Rican and a union organizer.

Someone I did not expect to see at this meeting was Efrain "Frank" Ramirez, Tito's brother-in-law, who unlike the rest of us, was neither an activist nor an organizer. Still, after hearing about the case, Frank had decided to join us because he believed nobody should ever be convicted unless proven guilty.

"According to these documents, Rolando's sentence has been appealed, so I'm not sure if there's anything we can do right now. As for Alex, we should find out if he needs a lawyer to appeal his conviction," proposed Margo opening the meeting.

"Let's meet with one or two lawyers who know the case," suggested Meca. "We could have a whole day retreat, maybe on a Saturday."

Meca's motion was unanimously approved. In the days that followed, we called the lawyers on the list I had gottten from Vicente and on a balmy Saturday afternoon in mid September 1991, we gathered once again at Tito's agency. The retreat proved to be very informative. Two of the three lawyers who made the presentation had defended Rolando in previous years. The third one, Michael Matnick, had represented Alex at his second trial. My first impression of the attorneys was that they still were very committed to proving the innocence of Cruz and Hernandez, possibly out of frustration with a reactionary criminal justice system that had entrapped their clients in a legal cat-and-mouse game.

At the end of the half-day retreat, we agreed to form the "Coalition for Justice," but most importantly, we vowed to bring the saga of Alex Hernandez and Rolando Cruz to the Latino neighborhoods of Chicago.

Chapter II

The Confession of Error

"Wrong is wrong, no matter who does it or who says it."
—Malcolm X

AT THE RETREAT THE LAWYERS agreed to support our organizing efforts with legal advice. Marlene Kamish, an energetic attorney acquainted with the case, volunteered for the job. Two weeks later, we gathered in Tito's office for the Coalition's official first meeting.

As we were walking into the conference room, the phone rang. "It's Marlene," I paused. "She's stuck in traffic."

"Don't you think that she behaves more like an activist than a lawyer?" ventured Tito as we waited.

To a certain extent, she did, maybe because she was a public defender who represented indigent death row inmates, or maybe because, like us, she had an insatiable appetite for justice. Still, I reminded Tito that from the first day we met, Marlene had made it clear that our success promoting justice for Rolando and Alex would depend highly on our ability to understand the workings of the criminal justice system.

"Sorry I'm late," said Marlene making her way into Tito's conference room. "This is a copy of Rolando's appeal brief that is pending before the Illinois Supreme Court," she added tossing what looked like a telephone book on the table. "If this court supports his death sentence, Rolando's life will be in grave danger," she continued, noting that, unlike the Illinois Supreme Court, which was compelled to hear all death penalty cases, the U.S. Supreme Court – at the last step of the appellate ladder – could refuse to review the case.

"Is there anything that we, as activists, or better yet, as 'the people' can do to influence the Illinois Supreme Court?" asked Meca.

According to Marlene, very little. "Other than what's been done already, filing an '*amicus brief*,' or a 'friends of the court brief,' which is what Cardinal [Joseph] Bernardin and other prominent people just did, I can't think of anything else. At least until this court decides to either uphold or overturn Rolando's sentence," she added.

"What about asking the DuPage state's attorney not to fight the appeal?" proposed Carlos.

"Because this is a capital case, a death penalty case, it's now up to Roland Burris, the [Illinois] attorney general, to argue for the prosecution," noted Marlene.

"Then, what about asking the attorney general to refuse to continue the case against Rolando?" Carlos seemed excited with this scenario. "After all, he's an African American and a Democrat."

"Yeah, but like Jim Ryan, he wants to go for higher office," reflected Pablo. "I bet you that in 1994, Ryan will run again for attorney general and Burris will seek the gubernatorial nomination," he added.

"I don't care about Burris' political ambitions," I protested. "Right now he is the state's top attorney. If he finds that Rolando was not duly prosecuted by Jim Ryan, I'm sure he has the responsibility to let the Supreme Court know, am I right?" I asked looking at Marlene.

"Absolutely," she said with a smile. "In fact, Burris could even ask the Justices to remand the case for a new trial."

"Then, let's meet with him," suggested Margo.

"It's somewhat tricky," cautioned Marlene. According to the law, Burris could ask the Supreme Court to grant Cruz another trial if he believed that the jurors had been denied the opportunity to hear exculpatory evidence that would have allowed them to reach a different verdict.

"If I'm not mistaken, I read somewhere that a juror at one of the trials said exactly that," started out Efrain paging through newsclippings. "Here it is, a juror who publicly admitted that if she had been allowed to hear evidence about Dugan's other crimes, she would have acquitted Alex at his second trial."

"What about the misleading evidence? What would have happened if DuPage prosecutors had told jurors the true size of the shoes that left the imprints under the window?" asked Tito.

"There are two things Burris could do about that," said Marlene. "One is to 'confess error' by pointing at mistakes made during the trial, either by the prosecutors, by the judge or by Rolando's lawyers, which may have prevented him from getting a fair trial. The other one is to start an investigation of misconduct against DuPage prosecutors for failing to turn key evidence over to the defense," she added.

"What about the boot print that they first tried to pin on Buckley?" interrupted Carlos. "I understand that at Rolando's second trial, DuPage prosecutors suggested it could belong to him."

"Right. Not only that, but did you know that when Dugan confessed to kidnapping Jeanine Nicarico in 1985, long before Rolando's second trial, he said that to gain access to the house he had kicked the door not once but twice?" Marlene paused, "and that his statement was corroborated by the FBI?"

The bewilderment in our faces said it all. According to Marlene, in June of 1986, as Buckley sat in a DuPage cell waiting to be retried and Cruz and Hernandez faced the death penalty, the Federal Bureau of Investigation not only had supported the conclusion that the boot print did not belong to Buckley, but had confirmed Dugan's statement that he had kicked the door of the Nicarico's twice. "Shortly after, Jim Ryan dropped all the charges against Buckley without offering any explanations," concluded Marlene.

"But he retried Cruz and Hernandez despite Cisowski's warning that Dugan might be guilty," added Tito.

"Could Burris also use the handling of the boot print evidence to bring charges of prosecutorial misconduct?" asked Carlos.

"Of course," replied Marlene.

In a way, a precedent had been set in 1988, when Buckley had filed a lawsuit against several DuPage law enforcement officers for conspiring to convict him based on the same boot print.

"What about the girl's size 6 shoeprints?" asked Margo.

Marlene nodded. "There were two prints, different shoes, right under 'the only window that was not covered by drapes, the only window that provided a clear view into that home,'" she said paraphrasing what DuPage prosecutor Richard Stock had told jurors at Rolando's second trial. What was important about Stock's remarks, added Marlene, was that on this occasion, he and his colleague, Robert Kilander, instead of denying Dugan's participation, were trying to tie Dugan to Cruz. "They wanted jurors to believe that Dugan and Cruz were accomplices. What they did not tell the jurors was that the prints belonged to girl's size 6 shoes and were much too small for either Cruz or Dugan."

As I also remembered, DuPage prosecutors knew from the start that the shoeprints did not belong to Cruz because, as it is common practice during any investigation, they had collected the shoe sizes of all major suspects before even charging them. Still, six years later, they had managed to convince jurors that one of the shoeprints could belong to Rolando.

"Is this an example of prosecutorial misconduct, or of incompetence from Rolando's attorney?" Meca's question caught Marlene by surprise.

"Whatever the case, it would allow Burris to 'confess error' and ask the Supreme Court for a new trial," replied Marlene.

Her point was well taken. Now we knew that Burris had at his disposal the legal tools to right a wrong and get an innocent man off death row. The lack of physical evidence and eyewitness testimony linking Rolando to the rape and murder of Jeanine Nicarico, coupled with the fact that the prosecution's case against Cruz was based mostly on the hearsay testimony of jailhouse snitches, should be more than enough.

Based on our conversations with Marlene, we agreed to ask for a meeting with Burris before the year's end. As we were leaving Tito's office, she offered to write a letter introducing the attorney general to the legalese of our request while we vowed to tap into a broader segment of the Latino community to make the meeting happen.

"I'll call the national organizations," volunteered Margo, whose father, longtime activist Bert Corona, was the founder and president of the advocacy group based in California she represented in the Midwest.

"I'll deal with the Puerto Ricans," offered Hector, who as the director of community affairs for the Commonwealth in Chicago, was highly regarded even by the most conservative people in his community.

"I'll help," added Meca, not only one of our greatest and most progressive leaders but the founder of the Segundo Ruiz Belvis Cultural Center, a magnet for youngsters in the Humboldt Park neighborhood.

"The 8th Day Center for Justice represents more than 20 religious communities," said Jean. "Do you want me to contact more groups? I'm afraid if I do, the Coalition will look like a congregation," she quipped.

"We need the religious leaders to protect us from evil, but we don't want to be drafted," quipped back Tito, who instead offered to recruit chambers of commerce and other groups that served the business sector because "they should also do what's right for the community."

As Jean and I agreed to help Marlene draft the letter to Burris, Carlos, in turn, proposed to call the leaders of the agencies that served the mostly Mexican-American Pilsen and Little Village communities.

Less than a week later, we had garnered the support of ten new organizations. "This case may well go down in Illinois criminal law history as one of the most controversial, political and unjust cases ever," we warned Burris in our letter. "We understand that the Attorney General has far reaching powers, including the power to order an investigation of prosecutorial misconduct, as well as the duty to confess error when appropriate," we charged.

Our letter seemed to work. At least that is what I thought when on November 18, 1991, I met other Coalition members in the lobby of the Thompson Center, the state building in downtown Chicago. As I rode the open elevator to the attorney general's office on the 12th floor, I remember feeling confident about the outcome of the meeting. That feeling, however, was short-lived. As we waited in the attorney general's conference room, a secretary came in and told us that due to his busy schedule Burris would not be able to join us. Instead, she said, we would be meeting with first Deputy Attorney General Joseph Claps.

"As we said in our letter, we're here to ask the attorney general to 'confess error' and to start an investigation of prosecutorial misconduct against the DuPage officials who were involved in the arrest and prosecution of Rolando Cruz," I started out, unperturbed by Burris' absence.

"We can't discuss the particulars of the case," replied a predictable Claps.

"So why are we here?" charged Carlos, playing the role of provocateur.

"At least you must agree with us that there is no physical evidence connecting Cruz to the Nicarico murder," pressed Margo.

Before Claps had a chance to give us another evasive answer, I intervened. "We want Mr. Burris to consider the option of asking the state Supreme Court to remand Cruz's case for a new trial," I told Claps as I gave him a list of more than 20 cases in which the Illinois attorney general's office had confessed error in recent years.

"And we want your office to investigate our concern that DuPage prosecutors and investigators might have mishandled evidence and threatened witnesses," said Pablo.

"That's right. The same way this office investigated Commander Cisowski after Jim Ryan accused him of feeding information to Dugan to validate his confession," added Tito.

"As you know, the investigation against Commander Cisowski was dropped," replied Claps defensively.

"But Cisowski's example proves that your office can conduct an investigation against a state law enforcement official, even in the middle of a case," pushed Hector.

This time, Claps did not say a word. Bringing the meeting to a close I decided to send Burris a strong message. "We're in no way satisfied with this meeting," I stressed before leaving. "And you can tell the attorney general we won't be satisfied until we discuss our concerns directly with him."

But before we had a chance to request another meeting with Burris, his office became engrossed in internal turmoil. In March, 1992, Assistant Attorney General Mary Brigid Kenney, who had been assigned to write the state's position on Rolando's appeal, resigned from her job claiming that she could not be part of the prosecution of an innocent man. Echoing our plea, in her letter of resignation, Kenney urged Burris to acknowledge before the Supreme Court the 'numerous' errors she had identified in the Cruz prosecution.

"We have to make public our meeting with Claps and our own demands regarding the case in solidarity with Kenney and to show that we're on the right track," proposed Hector as soon as we heard of the resignation.

A few days later, more than twenty Coalition members gathered in the lobby of the Thompson Center to demand an investigation of the DuPage authorities involved in the prosecution of Rolando Cruz. The previous weekend, we had collected more than a thousand signatures in support of our request, after speaking at two Catholic churches in the heavily Latino neighborhoods of Pilsen and Humboldt Park. "It was first communion Sunday," recalled Jean. "Yet, parents stood in line patiently in the cold to sign the petitions while their children waited in the church basement to have their communion breakfast."

"People in our community know that the Cruz and Hernandez case is about justice and not about trying to free two murderers, like some people in DuPage want us to believe," Tito told a reporter as we headed to Burris' office to deliver the petitions.

This time, I thought, the strategy really seemed to work. Less than a month after Kenney's resignation, Burris agreed to meet with us. Still, some in the Coalition dismissed the meeting as a political ploy.

"He's already said publicly he won't to do anything," complained Carlos.

"He can still change his mind," suggested Jean. "As an African-American politician, Burris has to be aware that no matter what he does to please the Democrats in downstate Illinois, he will never win the party's gubernatorial nomination unless he courts the minority vote," she ventured.

"He won't do it," predicted Pablo. He was right.

"A jury has found this individual guilty and given him the death penalty. It is my role to see to it that it's upheld. That's my job." As he spoke, Burris seemed to be reading from a carefully drafted script.

"But we gave your deputy, Mr. Claps, a list of cases in which attorneys general right here in Illinois have confessed error," I protested.

"The only way I would consider confessing error is if Cruz's lawyers can come up with new exculpatory evidence," he offered.

"Dugan's criminal history is exactly that," I pressed. "Besides, Mr. Attorney General, look at all the witnesses who have already recanted their testimony," I added.

Burris dismissed my claims saying I was bringing him just "hearsay evidence."

"Hearsay evidence is the only thing DuPage has against Cruz and Hernandez," I countered.

"You have the obligation to see that justice is done," interrupted Carlos, firm in his role as a no-nonsense activist. "Even jurors have admitted that if they had been allowed to hear about Dugan's criminal past, they wouldn't have convicted Cruz or Hernandez. We understand why DuPage may want to keep that evidence out of the courtroom. After all, Dugan was under their noses and they let him go. But we certainly can't understand why you don't want to do anything about it," Carlos challenged him.

Burris did not reply. It was obvious that he was becoming increasingly uncomfortable but it was also obvious that he was not going to change his mind. Still, I attempted to reach out to him just one more time. "Mr. Attorney General, we're asking you to investigate Jim Ryan's handling of this case as a group of concerned citizens," I pleaded.

"Right now, my office is involved in the prosecution of Rolando Cruz. We can't investigate allegations of misconduct against prosecutors whose judgement we are upholding," he replied.

"O.K. Then stop the prosecution of Rolando Cruz and ask the Supreme Court to grant him another trial," blurted Tito.

"Mr. Burris, you just mentioned a key word – judgement," insisted Jean. "As Illinois' top lawyer, you can exercise your own. You don't need to follow anyone else's."

"We're here because we know you can do it," added Carlos, pounding on the conference table.

"What Carlos means, Mr. Attorney General, is that we hope that your inability to confess error or to investigate DuPage is based on the law and not on politics," warned Pablo as it became obvious that the meeting had come to an end.

If nothing else, Pablo's remarks seemed to make an impression on Burris' chief of staff, Frank Nowicki, who offered a last minute recommendation. "If you believe there's been prosecutorial misconduct, you should ask the U.S. Department of Justice to investigate," he suggested.

"Why the Department of Justice, when your office can do it right now?" insisted Carlos.

"Because as I said, my job is to uphold the jury's decision to convict Mr. Cruz," intervened the attorney general. "Believe me, if there were something I could do, I would do it," he added sympathetically as we shook hands.

As I left his office, I hoped Burris would soon realize there was something he could and should do, particularly if in less than two years he expected to count on the Latino vote.

CHAPTER III

Exploring Federal Intervention

"The legitimate object of government is to do for a community of people, whatever they need to have done, but cannot do at all, or cannot so well do for themselves, in their separate and individual capacities."

—Abraham Lincoln

AFTER OUR MEETING, Hector and I headed to the Chicago-Kent School of Law to participate in a forum on the Nicarico case sponsored by the school's Hispanic Law Students Association. As we walked into the auditorium, I noted that it was packed with legal personalities, including Alex' current lawyer and renowned writer, Scott Turow.

When it was my turn to speak, I took the opportunity to discuss the implications of the case in the Latino community. "The Coalition believes that the number of Latinos who go through the criminal justice system will continue to rise. Therefore, we want to make sure that the rights of our people are always respected during their arrest, throughout their prosecution, and even after they're incarcerated," I told the audience.

As for Hector, he undertook a more proactive role, urging students to devote time and expertise to this and other cases involving our community. "Being a Latino should not pose a burden on your professional lives. On the contrary, it should allow you to better understand the needs of your community when confronted with the criminal justice system," he said.

Hector's remarks did not go unnoticed. The next day, the Chicago Sun Times reported that some of the students at the forum had volunteered to help with Hernandez's appeal by doing legal research for Turow. "At least the whole day was not a complete waste," said Hector when I called him about the article.

Days after our meeting with Burris, Charlie Kyle, our latest addition, endorsed Nowicki's suggestion to seek help from the U.S. attorney's office. "In fact, I think it's a great idea. Every time Cesar Chavez felt overpowered by the growers in California, he requested the assistance of the Justice Department," explained Charlie, whose own experience included working with the founder of the farm workers' movement. "Particularly if the situation involved a violation of civil rights, as seems to be the case here," he added.

Marlene was receptive but unsure about the timing of the proposed strategy. "Because the cases are still open, I don't know what the Department of Justice can do. Let me call a couple of lawyers who are experts in federal law and get back to you," she proposed.

"Even if, legally speaking, there were grounds for a federal investigation, aren't we naive to expect U.S. Attorney Fred Foreman, a Republican, to investigate Jim Ryan, not only another Republican, but one from DuPage?" asked Bob, well aware of the county's political clout.

"Regardless of his political affiliation, Fred Foreman must abide by the law," rebutted Hector carefully choosing his words, "So if the law says we have the right to seek federal relief, he'll have to let us know."

"Hector is right," agreed Jean. "This case is not about finding a politically correct way out for Rolando and Alex, but about uncovering the truth," she warned.

"This reminds me of a phrase of Cesar Chavez," added Charlie underscoring the importance of Jean's remarks. " 'Truth gets better with time.' So if we believe Rolando Cruz and Alejandro Hernandez are innocent, the longer we stay with the case, the more things will unravel," he predicted.

"If you meet with Foreman, I think there's a lawyer who would love to go with you," said Marlene, warming up to the idea.

A few days later Marlene called to give me the go-ahead. "By the way, the name of the lawyer is Gary Johnson. He's the Kane County state's attorney, he's a Republican, and what is most important, he was Buckley's defense lawyer at his defunct trial," she added.

Foreman did not keep us waiting. On April 15, 1992, less than a month after our ill-fated meeting with Burris, Hector, Tito and I arrived in the U.S. attorney's office, where we were met by Johnson. As Marlene had told us, the Kane County state's attorney was a Republican who had, in the past, shared a close friendship with Jim Ryan. Yet, soon after we met, Johnson explained that their relationship had soured when as Buckley's lawyer he had reminded the DuPage state's attorney that it was a prosecutor's job "to seek justice and not just to win convictions."

"Should we ask Foreman to appoint a special prosecutor based on our belief that Jim Ryan violated Rolando's and Alex' civil rights?" asked Hector.

"Just tell him what you told me – that you believe DuPage prosecutors and investigators have conspired to violate Cruz's and Hernandez's rights," he replied, stressing the importance of using the word conspire.

"Can Foreman refuse to intervene, like Burris did?" asked Tito, whose apprehension was understandable.

"Don't worry. With me in the room, at least he won't be evasive," replied Johnson.

A secretary interrupted to let us know that the U.S. attorney was waiting. Unlike Burris, who had met with us surrounded by staffers, Foreman was only accompanied by his second in command, Deputy U.S. Attorney Joan Bainbridge Safford.

Johnson's presentation was brilliant. He summarized the case in less than a few minutes using Dugan's confession as the centerpiece of his arguments. Why wouldn't Jim Ryan agree to give immunity to the convicted murderer in exchange for a full confession, he asked Foreman, when states' attorneys in two counties had done exactly that to secure Dugan's admission to the killings of Donna Schnorr and Melissa Ackerman?

"Well, I'm not in a position to second-guess the DuPage state's attorney, but it is my understanding that his office doesn't believe Dugan's confession to the Nicarico crime is acceptable," replied a cautious Foreman.

"As you know, Mr. Foreman, Jim Ryan personally asked State Police Commander Ed Cisowski to conduct an independent investigation of Dugan's confession," said Hector cutting into the discussion. "And at the end of his investigation, Cisowski told Ryan that despite a few inconsistencies, he was convinced that Dugan knew intimate details related to the kidnapping and killing of Jeanine Nicarico that only the murderer could know."

"Besides," interrupted Tito, "there's a witness who placed Dugan near the Nicarico home the day of the murder and two tollway workers who testified seeing a car similar to Dugan's leaving the scene of the crime," he noted.

"And while DuPage prosecutors hinted at Cruz's second trial that Dugan might be involved in the crime with Cruz and Hernandez, that is hard to believe knowing that Cisowski interviewed close to 80 people who knew the three men and came up empty handed looking for a link," I emphasized.

"What we can't understand, Mr. Foreman, is Jim Ryan's insistence not to plea bargain with Dugan even after two other state's attorneys have already granted him immunity," insisted Tito, stressing the fact that Ryan's refusal weakened Cruz's and Hernandez's chances of being exonerated.

"Besides, Jim Ryan's claims that Cisowski or anyone else could somehow have fed information to Dugan is not only ludicrous but raises serious questions as to the state's attorney's motives in requesting the independent investigation in the first place," I charged.

"I truly understand your concerns," said a polite Foreman. "However, two of the DuPage prosecutors who worked on the case, Tom Knight and Pat King, work for me now. So it would be a conflict of interest for my office to review your claims," he explained.

"Are you telling us that because two of the people involved in the case work in this office we have no legal recourse?" started Hector defiantly.

"No, by no means," intervened Foreman's deputy, Bainbridge Safford. "If you believe the rights of Cruz and Hernandez were violated, you are entitled to file a civil rights complaint with the U.S. Department of Justice in Washington, D.C."

"But before they agree to investigate, the Department of Justice must find clear evidence that DuPage prosecutors, police, or both, purposely violated Cruz's and Hernandez's civil rights," emphasized Foreman.

A week after our meeting with the U.S. attorney, I drove to Northwestern University to ask defense attorneys who had been involved in the case to help us launch the federal complaint.

"They're ready for you," said Marlene leading the way into a room filled with people.

"Do you know that these cases are very hard to prove?" asked Larry Marshall, Rolando's appeal lawyer, whom I recognized from the retreat.

"I understand that the FBI would first have to find proof that DuPage prosecutors and investigators did something wrong before they can be charged," I said casually.

"Do you also understand that they will have to find proof that for example, witnesses were forced to testify against their will or that DuPage prosecutors may have destroyed evidence?" asked Marshall.

"If I'm not mistaken, there are witnesses who have already admitted they were threatened by DuPage investigators into testifying against Rolando and Alex and later recanted their original testimony," I challenged. "And what about DuPage prosecutors knowing that the shoeprints found outside the Nicarico house were not Rolando's and telling jurors they were?"

Marshall seemed reluctant to embrace the federal strategy. Yet, he was careful not to step into the role of an activist. "I'm sure you and the Coalition will do what is best for Rolando," he said as the meeting came to an end.

"As you know, our number one priority is to get Rolando and Alex freed," I told him before we shook hands.

"How did the meeting go?" asked Margo a few days later as we gathered in Carlos' office.

"He didn't say so, but I believe Larry Marshall would prefer us to keep on putting pressure on Burris," I said.

"Doesn't he know that Burris gave us the runaround, twice?" asked Carlos.

"I'm sure he does," I said.

"O.K. Let's try again, but first let's bring Burris more petitions," proposed Tito. "Maybe when he starts counting, he'll come to his senses," he quipped.

Reluctantly, Carlos agreed. "But if it doesn't work, we'll do things our way," he warned.

Before we could approach Burris, fate intervened. This time, it was a divided Illinois Supreme Court that, in a 4-3 decision, narrowly upheld Cruz's death sentence arguing that his guilt had "been established beyond a reasonable doubt" and that Dugan's statements were both untrustworthy and inadmissible in a trial.

Writing on behalf of the three dissenting justices, Chief Justice Benjamin K. Miller, stated just the opposite. "Cruz's statements regarding the case are less detailed and specific than the statements made by Brian Dugan, who, unlike the defendant, provided law enforcement authorities with a confession of guilt for the offenses," he wrote.

Again, Brian Dugan stood at the center of the controversy.

Two days after the December 6th Supreme Court decision, we met to discuss what we thought was a terrible blow to justice. "Now is the time to stand up for Rolando and Alex and tell the whole world we won't give up until they're freed. Let's have a press conference in the lobby of the Thompson Center to say just that," urged Pablo.

On December 18, 1992, like soldiers who have been defeated in battle but still believe they are fighting the right
war, we responded to the court's decision with a message
filled with solidarity and defiance. "Today, we are here to
restate our commitment to pursue justice for Rolando Cruz
and Alejandro Hernandez. In doing so, we will continue to
raise the public's interest in their case and most important,
we will make sure that they are not forgotten just because
they are poor and Latinos."

CHAPTER IV

The March to Springfield

"In a democracy, dissent is an act of faith."
—J. William Fulbright

DURING THE CHRISTMAS HOLIDAYS, Charlie and I, now married, had come up with a plan to support a new trial for Rolando. "We think a march to the Illinois Supreme Court will get the attention of the new Justices," I said as we met in Tito's office in early January of 1993.

"Due to the general elections, three out of the seven Illinois Supreme Court Justices who were involved in last year's ruling left the bench," added Charlie. "So if the newly installed court agrees to revisit the case, and if this time they rule in Rolando's favor, at least he'll get another chance," he concluded.

Sally Reyes, a Puerto Rican business leader and a new member of the Coalition, immediately endorsed the idea. "As members of a democracy, we have the right to express our beliefs. Besides, the Supreme Court is empowered by the people, not by some divine energy," she quipped.

"Should we ask national leaders like Cesar Chavez to participate?" asked Tito.

"I don't know if we want to go national right now," replied Charlie. "One thing we do need is the help of people like Frank McNeal, the first African-American alderman in Springfield whom I've known since my days in the legislature, to make sure the march is not blocked by the police."

"Still, we should involve our legislators, both state and federal, maybe through a press conference," insisted Pablo, who thought that including the Latino political leadership in our strategies would considerably enhance our efforts.

As I looked around the room, I felt pleased with the many talents of the people who were part of the Coalition for Justice. In less than six months we had grown considerably to reflect the ethnic, social and economic diversity of the Latino community. Among us there were strategists, grassroots organizers, business leaders and political pundits. And as a bonus, Sister Jean represented the blessings and the support of more than twenty religious congregations.

"Diana and I have brought copies of a planning draft we prepared during our vacation," Charlie continued. "The draft includes ideas for the march and for a non-binding resolution calling for the legislature to ask the Supreme Court to reverse itself."

"What's a non-binding resolution?" asked Carlos.

"It's a public expression of endorsement by legislators, a symbolic gesture of their support for a person or an event." While working toward his doctorate, Charlie had served as an aid to the past president of the Illinois Senate, Philip Rock. In that capacity, Charlie himself had been the recipient of a resolution acknowledging his "outstanding service to the people of the state of Illinois."

"If we're going to do something like this, we need to have at least Miguel and Chuy on board," noted Bob referring to Senators Miguel del Valle and Jesus Garcia, our two highest ranking state officials.

"Let's think this through carefully. In order to introduce even a non-binding resolution, you need the support of the leader of either the Senate or the House," said Margo slowly. "Forget about the Senate. Republicans rule, so Miguel and Chuy won't do. While the House is still in the control of Democrats, if we need a Latino to introduce it, I don't see Miguel Santiago or Ben Martinez volunteering for this one," she said alluding to our senior state representatives.

"I think a couple of us should still meet with either Ben or Santiago and see what happens." I looked around the room for volunteers.

"Diana and I will do that," offered Tito, drafting me.

"In the meantime, we need some people to work on the march," pressed Sally.

"We should hold it sometime during the week of March 22. Although Rolando's sentence has been appealed by the lawyers, it's still the last date set by the Supreme Court for his execution," noted Charlie.

"We must be careful that whatever we do is not viewed as a political ploy or as some bleeding-heart liberals' attempt to oppose the death penalty," I cautioned. "We are a diverse group, so we have the respect of different constituencies, at least among Latino and religious communities," I mused.

"Let's face it, this case is very political," insisted Bob. "When they pinned the Nicarico murder on Rolando and Alex, Fitzsimmons and Jim Ryan were in the middle of an election," he pointed out.

"As for being a bleeding-heart liberal, nobody can accuse me of that," kidded Sally, a savvy businesswoman who counted among her friends several national Republican leaders.

Despite the lightheartedness of our discussion, we were aware that no matter what we did, some people would question our motives for helping Rolando and Alex because we were not lawyers, politicians or even their relatives or friends. "So why become involved?" many had asked me. The answer was simple. After ten years, it was obvious that the criminal justice system had failed these two men miserably. Today, it was Cruz and Hernandez. Tomorrow, it could very well be someone we knew.

"Before we move on the resolution, we'll need the blessings of [state Rep.] Michael Madigan, the speaker of the house," Charlie said. "So Tito and Diana have to get down to Springfield as soon as possible and, either through Ben Martinez or Miguel Santiago, find a way to get the Speaker's attention."

A few weeks later, we drove to the Capitol to meet with Ben Martinez, the Latino senior legislator and Madigan's close friend.

"I'll let him know you're here," said Ben's longtime assistant, Linda, as she saw us walk through the door. While we waited, Tito and I looked at the pictures of a smiling Ben shaking hands with mayors and governors. On a mantel, plaques from civic organizations stood as silent reminders of a life devoted to public service.

I was a little nervous about the meeting. After all, Ben was a conservative from the south side of Chicago who had rarely taken a liberal stand in his political life. I did not think it would be easy to have him introduce a resolution asking the House of Representatives to plead with the Supreme Court for the life of two Latinos convicted of a heinous crime. But as the senior legislator in the lower chamber, Ben was our only hope. Like Margo had predicted, although I hated to politicize Rolando's fate, the resolution had no chance of making it alive in a Republican-controlled senate whose leader, James "Pate" Philip, happened to be one of the most influential GOPers in DuPage and a close friend of Jim Ryan.

To my surprise, Ben was very receptive. "I've been following Cruz and Hernandez for a long time and I'm convinced this is the right thing to do," he said walking us to the door. "I'll ask Madigan to place the resolution on the agenda, but you'll have to lobby other Democrats to vote for it," he cautioned.

Feeling optimistic, Tito and I rushed through the corridors of the Capitol to share the news with Miguel del Valle and Jesus "Chuy" Garcia.

"What do you want us to do?" asked Miguel, visibly moved by Ben's decision to support the resolution.

"Join us at a press conference after the march and endorse the resolution," proposed Tito.

After getting the support of the Latino senators, Tito and I made our way to the Capitol cafeteria to meet with Gabriel Lopez, a friend and a lobbyist who had offered to help us get the votes to pass the resolution.

"The first thing you need to do is have community groups or churches in Madigan's district tell the Speaker they want the resolution placed on the agenda," he began.

"But we have less than two months," warned Tito.

"Gabe, as you probably know, Rolando's execution date has been set for March 22," I said elaborating on Tito's words. "So whatever we do between now and then should serve to call the Justices' attention to his innocence. We can't fail," I pressed.

Gabriel smiled briefly. "If you have enough voters who agree to call the Speaker, you won't, understand?"

We understood all right. Getting the resolution on the agenda would depend on how well we were at the political game. As hard as we tried to stay away from politics, it seemed to play a key role in our quest for justice.

Back in Chicago everybody was working on an assignment related to the march. Charlie was in charge of ensuring that the event complied with Springfield's city ordinances. As for Sally, she had been able to get local merchants to donate food for the trip while committing a Mexican-owned bus company to take our volunteers to the state capital.

On March 22, Rolando's assigned execution date and the day before the event, Charlie and I left for Springfield, carrying a list of 36 national and local community organizations, seven Latino elected officials and more than 25 religious congregations willing to support the resolution. Del Valle's assistant, Luz, had reserved the Capitol's pressroom where we planned to announce the legislative initiative right after the march. Once settled in our Springfield hotel, Charlie called Ald. McNeal to get his reassurance that the police would not disrupt the march.

The following morning, back in Chicago, a group of around 50 people met on the steps of the St. Sylvester church, in the Humboldt Park area. Holding signs that read, "We want a new and fair trial," they posed briefly for the media before climbing onto a double-decked bus.

"It was quite an experience," Sally mused upon her arrival in Springfield. "Most of our supporters are neighborhood people who made it all the way here, not to ask the legislature to give more money for their kids' schools, but because they don't want Cruz to die," she noted.

As we gathered in the Catholic cathedral in Springfield, we were joined by Alex Hernandez's parents, Haydee and Tomas and by Maria Rodriguez and her family, known in the Latino community for their beautiful songs and for their steadfast Christian devotion. "We want to let the attorney general and the members of the Supreme Court know that we have faith that justice will be done," said a joyous Maria as her musician-husband, Evaristo, hooked an electric guitar to the cathedral's sound system.

After a short prayer service led by John "Juancho" Donahue, the executive director of the Chicago Coalition for the Homeless, we walked toward the Illinois Supreme Court building escorted by a Springfield police car with lights flashing courtesy of Charlie's friend, Ald. McNeal. With everyone looking on in amazement, Tito stood firm in front of the building loudly appealing to the Justices' sense of fairness. In the background, Maria and her family sang a song asking God to give them wisdom and compassion.

As we made our way to the Capitol, we also stopped briefly outside Attorney General Burris' Springfield office. Maria's handpicked song about God's power to soften the human heart seemed particularly appropriate for this stop. "It may work," whispered Jean as she sang along.

Despite the bitter cold, our spirits remained filled with the warmth of hope. Slowly, we walked the otherwise deserted streets of Springfield singing songs and reminiscing about past rallies. "I can't believe we're still doing this. Do activists ever retire?" Tito quipped.

When we got to the Capitol, Senators del Valle and Garcia joined us at a press conference. "We want a justice system that works well for everyone," pledged Miguel.

"Given the doubt generated by Dugan's confession, I believe Cruz and Hernandez deserve new trials," proposed Chuy.

Del Valle and Garcia were not the only prominent Latinos endorsing our efforts. From Washington, U.S. Congressman Luis V. Gutierrez urged the Illinois Speaker to support the resolution. And through a written statement, Farm Workers' leader Cesar Chavez joined the Coalition "in calling for the Illinois Supreme Court to recognize the fact that these young men deserve a new trial and that the true perpetrator of the crime, Brian Dugan, must be charged for this crime in their stead."

A week after the march, Jean and I returned to Springfield to lobby for the passage of the resolution which had been given the number 333.

Two days after our visit to Springfield, Ben's assistant Linda called. "It looks like the Republicans are worried about the resolution," she said. "Madigan placed it on the agenda but Rep. Kathleen Wojcik, a Republican assistant minority leader from Schaumburg, asked that it be sent to committee. It's been assigned to Judiciary II, which deals with criminal justice."

This was not a good sign, I thought. According to Linda, non-binding resolutions were usually approved without any debate, but not in this case. "Ben has been scheduled to present it to the committee on April 1 and he wants you to testify," she said before she hung up.

"This gives us an idea of what we're up against," warned Carlos after I spread the news to the Coalition. "Or I should say, what Rolando and Alex are up against."

"Well, it's not that bad. Until now, we've been trying to avoid saying this case was political, but I guess the

Republican state representatives have taken care of that," said Sally with a sarcastic smile.

"Still, we must be careful not to make this is a partisan issue," I insisted. "Remember that one of the Justices who voted to remand Rolando's case for a new trial was a Republican. The same thing could happen again," I said, noting that toying with the political makeup of the court, even if we believed the odds would turn in Rolando's favor, was a dangerous affair. "We don't want to alienate anybody. I'm sure there are people in the Republican party who want justice for Cruz and Hernandez as much as we do. We must avoid politics at all costs."

Pablo agreed. "This case has more to do with incompetence and personal ambition than with political ideology."

"That's right. If, after the murder of Jeanine Nicarico, DuPage had looked into Dugan's record, Melissa Ackerman, the little girl he killed a year later, would probably be alive," I pointed out.

"Then, after Dugan confessed, Jim Ryan had already won office. So Cisowski's findings didn't fit his plans. After all, he had supervised the wrongful prosecution of three men. That wouldn't look too good in his resume," Sally reminded us.

"Going back to the resolution, in your presentation before the committee, make sure you quote law enforcement people like Cisowski and John Sam," suggested Margo.

In the days that followed, as I prepared to testify before the Judiciary Committee, I went over the names of law enforcement officials who had endorsed the innocence of Cruz and Hernandez. Former DuPage Sheriff's Detective John Sam, former DuPage Crime Lab Director Phil Gilman, former Illinois State Commander Ed Cisowski and former Illinois Assistant Attorney General Mary Brigid Kenney, they had all sacrificed their professional lives in the name of truth and justice. These people alone should be able to persuade everyone on the committee that Rolando deserves another chance, I thought.

Also revealing were the words from former Naperville Chief of Police James Teal that I spotted on a letter addressed to the judge who had presided over Alex' last trial. In his letter, the now retired chief of police admitted that, from the beginning, DuPage investigators and prosecutors had focused their attention on the two Latinos while being "unwilling or unable to consider other viable suspects and seek out invaluable physical evidence." This is exactly why Rolando and Alex are in this legal mess, I remember thinking as I put away Teal's letter.

Sorting through more pages of legal papers, I came across another letter to the same judge, signed by Jeremy Margolis, the former director of the Illinois State Police who had overseen Cisowski's investigation of Dugan's confession. "I share with a large number of Illinois State Police Officers the belief that Brian Dugan murdered Jeanine Nicarico and he did so acting alone," he wrote. Shaking my head in disbelief, I wondered how much higher on the law enforcement ladder I would have to go to convince the members of the committee that the

DuPage criminal justice system had made a terrible, but still reversible mistake.

CHAPTER V

The Resolution

"Justice is the end of government. It is the end of civil society. It ever has been and ever will be pursued until it is obtained or until liberty be lost in the pursuit."
— Alexander Hamilton

ON MARCH 31, as Charlie and I were leaving for Springfield, the phone rang. It was Linda. "There are nine Democrats and seven Republicans in the Judiciary II committee. The resolution needs at least nine votes. Ben says the Republicans will oppose it unanimously, which means that if a single Democrat takes a walk, it's all over."

It was obvious that someone wanted Resolution 333 killed. Fortunately, House Speaker Madigan, known in legislative circles as the "velvet hammer," never hesitated to exert his power for a good cause. Besides, Coalition supporters, including the retired nuns in the Speaker's district, had been flooding his office with letters and phone calls for the past month.

"Getting the nine Democratic votes shouldn't be a problem. We're on our way," I told Linda, hoping I was right.

Once in the car, Charlie and I discussed the phone call. "The Republican leadership must be trying to pressure Madigan to kill the resolution, but because the Speaker is also feeling the pressure from his constituency he's left the decision to the Democrats in the committee," speculated Charlie. "Linda's right. If one of them leaves the room when the votes are taken, it's all over."

"I'm sure there's at least one Republican willing to vote for the resolution," I insisted, still clinging to the idea that we should avoid partisan politics at all costs. "After all, it was a Republican Justice who supported Rolando's appeal and even wrote the brilliant dissenting opinion," I noted, referring to Benjamin Miller, the outgoing Illinois Supreme Court Chief Justice who had argued that Dugan was a credible suspect in the Nicarico crime.

Charlie disagreed. "No Republican in the committee will side with Justice Miller because he believes that evidence of Dugan's criminal past should be allowed at Rolando's trial. As we know, such evidence would show that unlike Cruz, Dugan has a history of raping and kidnapping young people dating from 1974. Because some of those crimes took place in DuPage County, and if I'm not mistaken, Dugan had been in a DuPage County cell days before abducting Jeanine Nicarico, this scenario doesn't make the county's criminal justice system look too good," concluded Charlie.

As I carefully considered Charlie's theory I realized he was absolutely right. Siding with the Justices who wanted to allow Dugan's other crimes into the courtroom was not a good political move for any Republican legislator who eventually would need the endorsement of the powerful party leaders from DuPage.

Therefore, neither was supporting Resolution 333, even when the initiative merely reiterated pleas from religious leaders and prominent attorneys, including several prosecutors. After all, if approved, Resolution 333 would deliver a public relations blow not just to the state's attorney's office and to the sheriff's department, but also to a county board that had authorized the spending of millions of dollars to repeatedly convict Cruz and Hernandez. "If the Nicarico murder had been committed in LaSalle County, like the Ackerman murder, Rolando and Alex would have been exonerated after Dugan's admission to the crime and millions of dollars in taxpayers' money would have been spared," I proposed.

"Unfortunately, it happened in DuPage County, home to Senate President James "Pate" Philip and to House Minority Leader Lee Daniels. That's why they're closing ranks," Charlie reminded me.

It was already midnight when we arrived in Springfield. After a few hours of sleep, Charlie and I headed to the Capitol to meet with Rep. Ben Martinez, the sponsor of the resolution. "I've talked to a lot of people and called in a lot of favors," he said as we walked toward the cafeteria before heading to the committee meeting. "I'm still not sure if the nine Democrats will vote as a bloc," he warned us.

Sipping my coffee, I tried to look calm while Ben discussed my testimony. "Your presentation must be brief, but it better be pretty convincing," he said with a smile.

Around 10:00 a.m., Charlie and I walked into a lively debate as members of the Judiciary II Committee considered supporting proposed legislation to curb domestic abuse. As we sat quietly in the back of the room I tried to focus my attention on the Democratic members, especially on Chairman Thomas Homer, who according to Ben, was committed to the resolution. As much as I tried, though, I could not keep Linda's warning out of my mind: "If one Democrat leaves the room, it's all over."

It was past noon before Homer asked Ben to address the audience. "They left the resolution for the end of the session, that's not a good sign," said Charlie as the Latino legislator waved for me to join him in the front of the room. As I started down the aisle, I saw a couple of Democrats heading out the side door. Linda's prediction was unfolding before my eyes. Suddenly, I noticed the would-be deserters were being blocked by the imposing figure of Rep. Edgar Lopez – one of Ben's closest allies. As soon as the two committee members realized what was happening, they looked at each other and without a word returned to their seats.

With all the Democrats and all the Republicans in the room, Homer called the meeting to order. Unexpectedly, a Republican committee member started reading a letter from Jim Ryan stressing that jurors at Cruz's last trial had been allowed to hear Dugan's confession to the Nicarico crime and that our resolution was baseless. "Wow, we must be rattling his cage" I whispered in Ben's ear. Nodding, Ben prompted me to contest Ryan's arguments.

"What the jurors were not allowed to hear were the details of the other two murders Dugan committed," I started, trying to control the nervousness in my voice. After all, it was the first time I had ever testified before a group of people powerful enough to vote on issues like the death penalty and mandatory sentencing. "Those details point out similarities in the killings of Jeanine Nicarico, Donna Schnorr and Melissa Ackerman," I went on, citing the jurors who had publicly admitted that if allowed to hear Dugan's criminal history, they would not have convicted either Cruz or Hernandez. "We, the people, believe that no one should be deprived of freedom unless there is absolutely no trace of reasonable doubt about the person's guilt," I said. "In Mr. Cruz's case, we believe that the amount of reasonable doubt is overwhelming."

Following my testimony, Rep. Tim Johnson, a Republican from DuPage, slammed a stack of unfinished paperwork on his desk charging disdainfully that "the Coalition has no business appearing before this committee."

Far from intimidating me, Johnson's theatrical display filled me with courage. "When the state kills, it kills in our name," I said slowly, savoring each and every word. "You represent the people and I am one of them. Therefore, I do have business here," I concluded looking defiantly into his eyes.

My remarks seemed to impress Rep. Rod Blagojevich, a Democrat from the northwest side of Chicago. Claiming to have been momentarily swayed by Johnson's arguments, he was the first one to exhort his colleagues to vote for the resolution because it was "the right thing to do."

But the most moving endorsement of our legislative initiative came from Committee Chairman Homer himself. "If I didn't support this resolution," he said, "I wouldn't be able to sleep at night." Simple, yet moving words, I thought.

Following Homer's call for action, Rep. Ray Frias, the only Latino in the committee seconded the motion. Then, one by one, the remaining Democrats joined them in voting for the resolution. As for the seven Republicans in the committee, they opposed it unanimously but unlike their colleague from DuPage County, quietly.

"This historic legislative effort will serve to document the support of the Latino community for Cruz and Hernandez," I told reporters as Reps. Ben Martinez, Ray Frias and Edgar Lopez, the resolution's improvised gatekeeper, looked on in approval.

A few days later, Charlie and I decided to bring the good news personally to Rolando, who for the past two years had been on death row at Menard Correctional Center, hoping for his sentence to be overturned. Tito and Efrain, who had just visited him, warned us against the trip. "The place is really scary," they said.

As we walked into the maximum security prison, I shrugged off my friends' remarks. "There's nothing unusual about this facility," I told Charlie as we gave our IDs to the security officer at the reception desk.

"Death row is up there," said the officer handing back our documents and pointing us in the direction of an old tower standing on a nearby hill.

The day was bright, providing a spectacular view of the river that surrounded the frightening complex. "Wouldn't it be beautiful to have a house with this view?" I said to Charlie almost in a whisper.

Once inside the tower, a narrow spiral staircase led us to a cafeteria equipped with vending machines. After stocking our trays, we kept climbing until we found ourselves in an enclosed space that looked like the catacombs. There, we were told to wait. Minutes later, Rolando arrived in his orange prison overalls, his head crowned in a colorful beaded cap. "I made it with the beads you sent me," he noted with a proud smile.

All and all, our visit turned out to be more pleasant than we had expected. Rolando had been allowed to bring pictures of his family and when we finished telling him about the trip, he started paging through a well-kept album, briefly pointing at a picture of a newborn baby. "This is my niece. She was born when I was already in jail," he said, his voice filled with sadness. "These pictures bring me closer to people I've never seen and to those I'll never see again," he went on, stroking a picture of his late father. "When he died, I was in prison and they wouldn't let me go to the funeral," he said.

"We just had Resolution 333 passed out of the judiciary committee and we're hopeful the Supreme Court will give you another trial," cut in Charlie in an attempt to cheer him up.

"The opposition was unbelievable, but it backfired," I noted, recounting my verbal duel with Rep. Johnson.

"We know that the Republicans oppose the resolution, so we don't expect it to get out of the House of Representatives alive," Charlie went on. "Still, our efforts were successful because they ignited public discourse. Now everyone knows that we, the people, support your innocence," he added.

As Charlie kept on talking about the Coalition's initiatives, Rolando became more animated. By the time he heard of Tito standing triumphantly on the steps of the Supreme Court building like a warrior emerging from the battlefield, I noticed that the young Mexican-American was laughing wholeheartedly.

Before leaving, Charlie and I assured him that we would continue to work hard until he and Alex were completely exonerated.

Once in Chicago, we gathered in Tito's office to discuss our next move. "No matter what happens in Springfield, I think we should keep working on our elected leaders," insisted Pablo albeit agreeing with Charlie that the resolution would not make it out of the House.

"If nothing else, our continuous lobbying will educate legislators and keep Dugan at the center of the case," said Sally supporting Pablo's strategy.

"It's important that we make people understand that, contrary to what Jim Ryan and his minions claim, the inconsistencies in Dugan's confession are insignificant compared to the lack of evidence against Alex and Rolando," I noted. "Besides, Dugan would be a fool to incriminate himself beyond a reasonable doubt without getting immunity," I added.

"That immunity deal is what worries me most of all," said Sally with a sigh. "Why does Jim Ryan continue to refuse doing what his colleagues in LaSalle and Kane already did?" she asked as if working her way through a puzzle. "I'm sure once granted immunity, Dugan will gladly provide DuPage prosecutors with all the evidence they need, like he probably did in the cases of Donna Schnorr and Melissa Ackerman."

"Let's also not forget that there are enough details in Dugan's confession that were unknown until he mentioned them. For starters, the kind of tape he used when kidnapping Jeanine," interrupted Meca, alluding to Dugan's description of a serrated-edged masking tape he said he had used to blindfold the Naperville girl. "This type of tape is no longer sold in stores but was available at the time of the murder," she reminded us.

"Or that he kicked the door of the Nicarico's twice," said Pablo, referring to the statement that Dugan had given DuPage prosecutors in 1985, almost a year before the FBI reached the same conclusion.

"Details that Dugan could not have picked up from media accounts," noted Tito.

"Or from Cisowski, as Jim Ryan inferred," I charged. "It's unbelievable that nobody has yet questioned this guy's motive for implying that the state investigator reinforced

Dugan's confession by feeding him information unknown to the public," I complained.

"And besides, in support of Cisowski's conclusion, what about the witness who saw Dugan near the Nicarico's the day of the crime?" asked Margo, alluding to the church secretary who had recognized Dugan by his drooping eyelid after seeing his picture on the news. According to the woman, Dugan had been in the vicinity of the Nicarico home just minutes before the abduction of the Naperville girl.

"Or the two tollway workers who not only described Dugan's car as the one leaving the scene of the crime but emphasized seeing only one individual, a white guy, in the vehicle," added Tito.

"We should have another petition drive in Pilsen and Humboldt Park and distribute all this information on Dugan," proposed Carlos.

"Good idea, and let's include his other crimes, which by the way took place mostly in DuPage and in neighboring Kane County," Meca pointed out.

"At this point, why not denounce a political cover up?" asked Pablo. "At least, we should publicize a couple of chronological coincidences that point in that direction. Take the indictments of Cruz, Hernandez and Buckley, for example. They took place just 12 days before Jim Ryan defeated Fitzsimmons in the Republican primary for state's attorney. I'm sure that both candidates must have discussed the crime on the campaign trail and that both must have promised to punish the perpetrators to the fullest extent of the law," he concluded.

"There's another interesting political coincidence surrounding this case," agreed Bob. "When Brian Dugan was charged for the murder of Melissa Ackerman in June 1985, Ryan had expressed his interest in getting the GOP nomination for attorney general," he remembered. "But, later that year, after Dugan's publicized confession of the Nicarico murder, Ryan mysteriously dropped his nomination, possibly to avoid the embarrassment of being asked about Dugan during the campaign."

As we continued our discussion, Efrain doled out news clippings that detailed Dugan's troubles with the law had started in 1974, when as a youngster he had allegedly raped a 10-year-old girl in west suburban Lisle. Between 1974 and 1982, the clippings showed, Dugan had continuously been in and out of prison on charges stemming from burglary to arson.

"Look at this," cried out Tito pointing to one account. "By the time La Salle County authorities suspected Dugan of killing 7-year-old Melissa Ackerman, Dugan was already in the Kane County Jail charged with the attack on two women and with the rape of another one in Aurora. And soon after, he was identified as a suspect in the one year-old-unsolved murder of Donna Schnorr."

"We should bring this information to Springfield and personally hand it to those who support Jim Ryan's position that there's not enough evidence to charge Brian

Dugan with the murder of Jeanine Nicarico," suggested Efrain.

"That's why even when we know the resolution will never make it to the full House for debate, we should stay with it," insisted Pablo.

Determined to keep Dugan at the forefront of the Nicarico case, Sister Jean and I volunteered to go to Springfield one more time. The Sunday prior to our trip, the Coalition held petition drives outside Catholic churches in the predominantly Latino neighborhoods of Humboldt Park, Pilsen and in suburban Aurora, where we were joined by friends and relatives of Rolando and Alex. In a few hours we collected thousands of signatures urging State Rep. Michael Madigan, as the Speaker of the House, to pass Resolution 333.

Once again people stood patiently in line, asking questions and signing petitions. One lady at St. Pious, a church in Pilsen, gave me her *bendición* and exhorted the Coalition to keep unraveling the controversial case. "Like Cesar Chavez used to say," she reminded me as we were leaving the church, "justice is not for sprinters but for long distance runners."

Sadly, days later, we got word that Cesar had died in Arizona. Shortly before his death, during a brief stop over in Chicago, this great national leader wrote us an encouraging message on the back of a manila folder: "I'm very hopeful justice will be done. Keep up the good work."

On May 4, 1993, Sister Jean, the Hernandezes and I met again in the Capitol corridors. As representatives came out of the legislative session, we handed them copies of the resolution and a letter from Haydee. "While at the beginning of the investigation Alex thought he was helping the police, he soon went from junior detective to murder suspect with the help of witnesses who later claimed they had lied under pressure from prosecutors," she began, recounting her son's ordeal.

In the letter, Haydee also explained that when Alex had been charged with the Nicarico crime, she had approached a DuPage prosecutor with proof that he was not in Naperville at the time of the crime. "I gave him a receipt from the store where Alex had been that day buying materials to rebuild our driveway," explained Haydee. "Later, at Alex' trial, he [the prosecutor] denied ever seeing the receipt and when I went to the store to get the merchant's copy, the owner told me it had already been claimed by DuPage investigators."

In closing, Haydee's letter made a compelling case for her son's innocence. "My husband and I are poor and honest people who have taught our children to love God and respect all living things," she wrote. "If we thought that our son was in any way related to such a terrible crime, we would disown him ourselves."

On May 12, as we had predicted, although Resolution 333 had been scheduled for debate, it was never called to the floor. "Well, at least we made enough noise in Springfield to hopefully reach even the ears of the Justices," Tito mused.

Less than two weeks later, in a unanimous decision, the Illinois Supreme Court agreed to revisit Rolando's case.

Chapter VI

The Illinois Supreme Court Hearing

"We must have strong minds, ready to accept facts as they are."
—Harry S. Truman

THE DECISION by the Illinois Supreme Court to rehear Cruz's arguments for a new trial was a step in the right direction. Yet, we at the Coalition doubted that the legal system alone would right the terrible wrong that had been perpetrated against him and against Alex Hernandez.

For more than ten years, justice had eluded the two Latinos while the DuPage state's attorney's office, led by Jim Ryan, continued to reinvent the crime scenarios to convict them. Had they committed the crime with Stephen Buckley or with Brian Dugan? Had Jeanine Nicarico been murdered on the Illinois Prairie Path, as prosecutors claimed earlier in the case, or had she been killed elsewhere, as they had told jurors at Cruz's second trial after Dugan admitted killing the little girl on the Path?

As long as Jim Ryan's office kept on presenting the crime so it would fit Cruz and Hernandez like the infamous size 6 girl's shoe, there would be no real justice. So far, neither the lack of evidence that had exonerated Buckley nor the physical evidence and witness testimony that pointed toward Dugan had brought any legal relief for either Latino.

"According to the lawyers, Rolando's appeal will be heard by the Illinois Supreme Court around June 20th," said Pablo as we gathered at a Puerto Rican restaurant to celebrate the high court's decision. "We need to meet again with Burris and this time convince him to confess error," he proposed, confident that following the Justices' unusual ruling, the state's top prosecutor would change his mind and forego pursuing Rolando's conviction.

At this juncture in the case, though, most of us adamantly opposed engaging in anymore dealings with the [Illinois] attorney general. "He's said a hundred times he'll uphold the conviction so I don't see why he would back off just because we ask him one more time," protested Carlos, convinced of Burris' determination to see the appeal through.

Unfortunately, until the Illinois Supreme Court decided whether to uphold Rolando's death sentence or grant him a new trial, there was little else that we, as advocates, could do. "Even Alex' appeal has been put on hold," pointed out Pablo, insisting on the strategy.

After a short deliberation, we agreed to give the attorney general another try. "Before meeting with Burris, let's discuss what we did at previous meetings so we don't use the same arguments," proposed Sally.

"At our first meeting with Claps, his deputy, we talked about the relevance of Dugan's confession to his other crimes, which is at the center of the appeal," recalled Jean. "When we met with Burris for the first time, we brought up Dugan again. This time we should try something else," she said.

"What about the DNA?" asked Margo, referring to the genetic testing that had revolutionized forensic technology.

Back in 1989, blood samples from Dugan, Cruz, Hernandez and Buckley had been sent to a laboratory in California to be matched with samples removed from Jeanine Nicarico's body. The testing had proved inconclusive for Rolando and had eliminated Alex and Buckley as potential rapists of the 10-year old girl. Dugan's sample, on the other hand, had closely matched the foreign material found at the crime scene.

Unfortunately, DuPage prosecutors had successfully argued against allowing the results into evidence and, because appeals can only deal with issues brought up during a trial, the DNA was out of the question. "Instead, let's discuss the evidence against Rolando," I proposed.

"What evidence? The prints under the window that proved to be from a girl's shoe or the boot print on the Nicarico's front door that they tried to pin on him after failing to prove it was Buckley's?" mused Tito.

"I'm talking about the third-party testimony that twice convinced a jury that Rolando committed the crime," I rebutted, alluding to the statements he had supposedly made to relatives and fellow inmates and to the "vision" about the murder that he had allegedly discussed with two DuPage investigators.

That "vision," I argued, seemed to be the most damning piece of evidence against Cruz, not so much for the accuracy of the statement as for the men who swore by it. Those men, DuPage Detectives Tom Vosburgh and Dennis Kurzawa, claimed that, in a "vision" statement, Cruz had revealed that Jeanine Nicarico had been abducted from her house wrapped in a blanket, that she had been sexually assaulted and that "she had been struck so hard that her head had dented the ground."

Despite its relevance, I pointed out, neither Vosburgh nor Kurzawa had told the DuPage state's attorney's office about the statement until 19 months later, almost on the eve of Rolando's indictment.

Besides, I reminded the group, there was also the testimony from dubious, yet convincing witnesses who had testified at Rolando's two trials. One of those witnesses, Cruz's cousin Ramon Mares, had originally testified that in 1983 Cruz had told him that he knew who had killed Jeanine Nicarico and that he, Cruz, had been present when the girl was killed. Shortly before Rolando's second trial, however, Mares acknowledged lying after prosecutors threatened him with perjury. According to news accounts, a polygraph test subsequently proved Mares' recantation to be true.

Another of the prosecution's "star" witnesses, I recalled, was Steve Pecoraro, a psychiatric inmate who had been convicted of stealing body parts. During the first trial, Pecoraro testified that Rolando had admitted participating in the murder with Alex Hernandez and Stephen Buckley. This testimony, however, contradicted Robert Turner's. Turner, a death row inmate, testified at Cruz's second trial that it was Dugan, and not Buckley, who Rolando had fingered as his partner in crime.

"Even DuPage prosecutors made contradictory statements, which if I'm not mistaken would amount to misconduct," added Tito, reminding us that at Cruz's first trial, DuPage prosecutors had tried to fit the bootprint on the Nicarico's door to Buckley. At Rolando's second trial, however, they had hinted that the print could have been made either by Cruz or Dugan.

"No matter how weak we think the evidence is against Rolando, Burris will continue to play the same record, that he must uphold the decision of the jurors who voted twice to convict him," interrupted Hector, paraphrasing the attorney general.

"If Burris wants to talk about jurors, let's bring him the statements from the ones who said they voted to convict Rolando and Alex because they believed in the testimony of the jailhouse snitches and the witnesses who later recanted," proposed Pablo, recalling one juror who had acknowledged that Cruz and Hernandez had been convicted because "half the population of East Aurora implicated the two defendants."

To prepare for our second meeting with Burris, scheduled for June 16, we agreed to ask Marlene to help us document our claims with court records or affidavits from witnesses who had recanted their testimony. "This time he won't be able to tell us we're bringing him gossip from newspaper clippings," I reflected.

Besides collecting legal ammunition, we summoned religious and Latino community leaders to blitz Burris' office with letters and phone calls asking him to confess error. One of those leaders was Fabio Naranjo, a member of the Attorney General's Hispanic Advisory Council – a group that advised Burris on issues relevant to the Latino community. In his letter, Naranjo alerted Burris to call a special meeting of the council because "careful delibera-tions of the moral arguments and political ramifications of this case should be within the purview of our task."

Unfortunately, neither Naranjo's letter nor our carefully drafted strategy had any effect on the attorney general, who, in closing the meeting, reiterated his decision to uphold Rolando's death sentence.

This time, though, we were left with a small victory. Shortly after, Burris' liaison to the Latino community, William Delgado, resigned partially due to the attorney general's position on the case.

On June 22, 1993, Charlie, Jean and I made our way through a packed courtroom in the Supreme Court build-ing in Springfield to witness Larry Marshall fight for his client's life.

Arguing there was neither physical evidence nor eyewit-ness testimony linking Rolando to the abduction or to the murder of Jeanine Nicarico, Marshall asked the Justices to carefully look at the evidence against Brian Dugan. Emphasizing that the murder of Jeanine Nicarico was a sexual crime and not a bungled burglary, the Northwestern University law professor also argued that Dugan's criminal record was essential to his client's defense.

The hearing reached its high point as one of the Justices asked Assistant Attorney General Terence Madsen why he believed Cruz's alleged "vision" was more accurate than Dugan's statements about the Nicarico crime. Madsen's answer, that Cruz's statements were more credible because "they came first," prompted Rolando's attorney to remind the prosecutor that they were not involved "in a race."

After the hearing, the three of us gathered at a nearby restaurant. "Madsen really did a very poor job trying to uphold Rolando's death sentence," commented Jean, pointing out that the assistant attorney general's admission that "some day, the state may prosecute Dugan for this crime," had been most revealing.

"To overturn Rolando's conviction, the Justices must find Dugan a credible suspect. By opening the door to the possibility of Dugan's involvement, Madsen might have inadvertently pointed them in that direction," agreed Charlie.

"If Jim Ryan had accepted Cisowski's conclusion about Dugan's guilt in 1987, Rolando would not even be in this legal mess right now," I noted.

"In any case, two out of the three Justices who ruled in Cruz's favor last December found Dugan's statements about the Nicarico murder more accurate than Rolando's questionable 'vision.' So, if at least two out of the three new Justices choose to support this theory, there will be enough clout to force Dugan's criminal past out into the open," concluded Charlie.

"Are you telling me that what these eminent jurists will be pondering is whether Dugan's other crimes are similar enough to the Nicarico murder to render any credibility to his confession?" asked Efrain when we met to discuss the Supreme Court hearing.

"Right. And, they will also weigh whether allowing Dugan to testify at Rolando's trial could hinder DuPage prosecutors from charging him at a future day," explained Jean.

"That won't be a problem if Dugan is treated as a witness at Rolando's next trial and charged with killing Jeanine Nicarico after Cruz is exonerated," noted Charlie.

"I wonder if the Justices would have upheld Rolando's death sentence had they been able to consider the DNA evidence," insisted Margo. If nothing else, she argued, the 1989 testing of genetic material that had placed Dugan among the 14.6 percent of the male population whose genetic type matched the semen found in Jeanine Nicarico' body was accurate enough to lend credibility to his confession.

Following the hearing, the high court recessed until September, leaving Rolando, and Alex by extension, in a legal limbo. Determined not to let people forget their plight for justice, Coalition members secured appearances on TV shows that dealt with Latino issues, like Channel 32's "*Entre Amigos*" and Channel 9's "*Charlando*." These venues, besides the local Spanish-language media outlets, allowed us to share with the Latino community the injustices that the DuPage criminal justice system had perpetrated against two of our own.

"We should have a press conference about Burris' refusal to confess error in light of the Supreme Court hearing," proposed Jean at a meeting to discuss future strategies. "People should know he refuses to acknowledge trial errors that, in the opinion of at least three Justices, should get Rolando another chance."

"Let's also publicize Madsen's comment that Rolando's 'vision' is more accurate than Dugan's confession because it came first," I proposed.

"And his attempt to undermine Dugan's history of sexual crimes when he said that only one of Dugan's other two murder victims was a child or that Dugan couldn't have kidnapped Jeanine Nicarico because he usually picked up his victims in public places," added Tito.

"What about Madsen's claim that Dugan couldn't have killed Jeanine Nicarico because she was bludgeoned to death while Dugan's other victims were drowned?" asked Sally.

On July 14, less than a month after the Supreme Court hearing, more than 30 representatives of Latino elected officials, religious and community organizations gathered in the lobby of the Thompson Center one more time. "We're here simply to ask for justice," said Zeferino Ochoa, executive director of the Chicago Archdiocese's Committee for Spanish Speaking Catholics. "Let's stop this case. It's the humane and logical thing to do," he demanded before the many reporters who had come to cover the event.

After the press conference, the entire group headed to the attorney general's office to tell Burris, for the last time, that as overseer of the system, he had the responsibility to seek justice, not just to uphold a dubious conviction.

As we were leaving his office, Maria D'Amezcua, a new Coalition member and the local president of the League of United Latin American Citizens (LULAC), threw a final warning at the attorney general. "This case is very important for the Latino community. To ignore our plea for justice is an irreparable and unforgivable mistake," she said.

Chapter VII

Two Life-Saving Decisions

"Morality may consist solely in the courage to make a choice."
—Leon Blum

Days after our visit to Burris' office, in an unprecedented move, the U.S. Supreme Court ruled that prosecutors could be sued for making public statements and for concocting physical evidence against Stephen Buckley, the third man who had originally been tried with Cruz and Hernandez in 1985. "This decision could guarantee that Rolando and Alex don't keep on riding a roller coaster of prosecutorial misconduct," predicted Jean. "We should meet with Flynt and find out more," she said alluding to G. Flynt Taylor, the civil rights attorney from the acclaimed People's Law Office who had won Buckley the right to sue.

"Two important things happened here," explained Taylor as Tito, Jean and I gathered in his office to discuss the ruling. "The first one is that the court unanimously reinstated the lawsuit we filed in 1988. That lawsuit, as you may recall, charged that DuPage prosecutors fabricated evidence to link the print on the Nicarico's front door to Stephen's boot."

"Yeah, they did such a good job that not even the jury bought it," Tito quipped.

"Still, they managed to keep Stephen in jail for almost two years," noted Taylor.

"You said there were two parts to this decision," said Jean, who was meticulously taking down every word.

"That's right. The U.S. Supreme Court has also ruled that Michael Fitzsimmons, the former DuPage state's attorney responsible for indicting Buckley with Cruz and Hernandez, could be liable for statements he made at the press conference announcing the charges," added Taylor.

"What bothers me is that everybody claims there's nothing political with this case," blurted Tito. "Meanwhile, Fitzsimmons announced the indictments days before the primaries. Jim Ryan, who wants to be attorney general, keeps on prosecuting Cruz and Hernandez and ignoring Brian Dugan despite Cisowski's conclusion that he killed Jeanine Nicarico and despite Dugan's record as a sexual offender. And Burris wants to reassure downstate voters that he's tough on crime so he can win the Democratic nomination for governor. Nooo, there's nothing political about this case."

Jean nodded in approval. "What impact, if any, could Buckley's decision have on Rolando and Alex?" she asked.

"Other than send a strong message to DuPage prosecutors, not much," said Taylor, "at least, until their trials are over." According to Taylor, although the U.S. Supreme Court would uphold Cruz's and Hernandez's right to sue for prosecutorial misconduct, they would not be able to exercise that option until they were both exonerated of criminal charges.

"If I'm not mistaken, former U.S. Attorney Fred Foreman told us we could ask for a federal investigation if we thought Rolando and Alex had been wrongfully convicted," remembered Tito.

"As a group, you can ask the U.S. Department of Justice to investigate violations of their civil rights if you have evidence of prosecutorial misconduct or if you fear for their safety," explained Taylor. "What we've won here today, is the right for Buckley to seek monetary compensation from those who put him behind bars despite the lack of evidence."

As we left the lawyer's office, I turned to Tito and Jean. "Now more than ever, I think that as soon as Rolando's sentence is overturned we should go to the Department of Justice."

"You seem pretty confident that this time the Illinois Supreme Court will grant Rolando a new trial," noted Tito.

"Yes, as I'm also confident that he and Alex will get out of prison. The question is, what can we do to make it happen sooner rather than later," I replied.

"We'll discuss it another time. Right now, we've got to run," said Tito as he waved goodbye to Jean.

"Where are you guys going?" she asked.

"We're heading downtown, to put the final touches on the upcoming 'Day of solidarity with Latino inmates on death row,'" I said. "Our position should be that we oppose the death penalty because it has been and still can be applied to innocent people like Rolando," I proposed.

"Despite my religious conviction that the death penalty is wrong, period, I think that your argument works well even among those who support it," cheered Jean as she got into her car.

Organizing a march and rally in the heart of the predominantly Mexican Pilsen neighborhood was not an easy task. Because we planned to walk along the busiest street in the area on a Saturday, we needed a city permit and assurance from the police that we would not be accosted by traffic. "As long as you get to Zapata Park around noon, it'll be O.K," said a representative of the police department who attended the meeting. "Make sure you don't engage in any arguments with onlookers," he warned us, probably unaware that most of the people in the area would be supportive of the event.

While Rolando was the perfect local poster boy against the death penalty, there were other Latinos in the country who had fallen prey of a criminal justice system prone to mistakes that could lead to the execution of innocent people; like Ricardo Aldape Guerra, a Mexican national convicted of conspiring to kill a Texas police officer even when he had no weapon and did not even know the guy who had pulled the trigger. "If there's one good solid argument against the death penalty," I said as we wrapped up the meeting, "it is that it offers no safeguards to prevent the killing of innocent human beings."

On August 14, a group of about 200 people peacefully congregated at the Emiliano Zapata Park on the West End of Pilsen, after marching for more than a mile down 18th Street. As we listened to the many speakers who had come from all over the country to support the rally, Maria and I stood next to each other, holding signs that read "Ten years of injustice for Rolando Cruz. Innocent and yet on death row!"

Meanwhile, six months had passed since Larry Marshall had argued Rolando's case before the Illinois Supreme Court and we were still awaiting a ruling. Eager to keep on promoting the innocence of Cruz and Hernandez throughout the Latino community, Maria, Jean and I accepted an invitation to appear on "*Mesa Redonda*," a local TV program on Spanish-language Channel 44.

Due to the popularity of the weekly show, we decided to announce our intention to seek federal relief while on the air. A day after the show, hundreds of calls flooded our offices. Some, from viewers who knew someone in trouble with the criminal justice system, others, from people who wanted to help. But what every caller agreed on was that if we did not keep on putting the Cruz and Hernandez case out in the public forum, it would be much harder for the two Latinos to get vindicated.

Early the following year, as the 1994 primary elections approached, the National Association of Latino Elected Officials (NALEO) held its annual national convention at the University of Chicago in Hyde Park. Salvador Cerna, the executive director of the agency's local chapter, asked Coalition members to address a gathering of young Latinos from all over the country who attended the conference. "I especially want you to review the Cruz and Hernandez case," said Salvador as we discussed our participation at the event. "These young people should know that it's possible to organize against the unfairness of the criminal justice system, to stand up against those who think we are disposable." Salvador's words reminded me of something Cesar Chavez had told Charlie days before his death. "If you don't put a stop to this injustice, unscrupulous prosecutors will assume that they can kill Latinos like flies."

The NALEO conference also gave us the opportunity to discuss two statewide upcoming elections. One was Illinois' gubernatorial primary, where Burris would face several tough opponents in his quest for the Democratic nomination; and the other one was the Republican primary for attorney general that would pit Jim Ryan against Jeff Ladd, the chairman of the train system Metra.

"In statewide races it is hard to trace the Latino vote down party lines. Still, the Coalition for Justice has already asked all our elected officials to withhold their support for Roland Burris and Jim Ryan," Maria told the crowd, explaining the impact of grassroots organizing in the political process.

While on the topic of how to exert power at election time, I was asked what party I thought better served the needs of the Latino community. "When it comes to issues like immigration and the death penalty, I believe the Democratic Party still carries the torch," I said. "As for the Republicans, they certainly represent the interests of Latinos on their way up. And they also represent family values, unless your family happens to be *mojada* (undocumented)."

"In the upcoming elections I predict that no Latino elected official will endorse either Burris or Jim Ryan," said Maria in closing. "Attempting to cash in on the prosecution of Cruz and Hernandez by claiming higher office might be O.K. with some people but to our community it's unacceptable," she concluded as hundreds of young Latinos honored us with a warm round of applause.

A few days after the NALEO conference, the Chicago Sun Times echoed Maria's pledge, endorsing Jeff Ladd over Jim Ryan in the primary race for attorney general. "Charges that Ryan mishandled the notorious Jeanine Nicarico case are too troubling to ignore, especially since they involve questions of whether an innocent man might be executed for the murder of the 10-year-old girl," they wrote.

Notwithstanding the editorial, on March 15, Jim Ryan comfortably won the Republican nomination for attorney general, partly due to his endorsement by the DuPage Republican machine. In the primary bid for governor, though, Latinos split their support between State Comptroller Dawn Clark Netsch, a brilliant politician from the liberal Chicago lakefront and powerful Cook County Board Chairman Richard Phelan.

As the primaries unfolded, Charlie and I took a one-day trip to the Pontiac Correctional Center to visit Alex. "We'll meet you in the parking lot," I told Haydee on a sunny Sunday morning before leaving for the three-hour ride.

As we were nearing Pontiac, I noticed I did not have my driver's license. "I can't believe I switched bags and forgot to check," I told Charlie almost in tears. "Without a photo ID, I won't be able to get inside."

My unfortunate mistake worked in Mr. Hernandez's favor, who was able to take my place and visit with his son. It was a beautiful day, so I opened the car's sunroof, turned on the radio and tried to make the best out of a long wait.

Two hours later, as Charlie and the Hernandezes emerged from the prison, I detected a gloomy look in their eyes. "What's going on? What happened?" I asked.

"Alex has been beaten," said Charlie. "Let's go some place where we can talk."

Seated at a nearby restaurant, Charlie and Haydee took turns telling me about the ordeal. A few days earlier, Charlie began, four intimidating-looking inmates had cornered Alex in a shower stall.

"One of them threw him a knife," interrupted Haydee, visibly upset. "But instead of picking it up, Alex kicked it away because he didn't want anyone to get hurt."

Safety concerns for Rolando and Alex had always been a priority for the Coalition. After all, if the two were killed, their innocence would become irrelevant. Alex was particularly vulnerable, I thought, because he had misconstrued his role in prison and believed he was there to "help the guards."

"I didn't want to tell you over the phone, but this is not the first time he's been harassed," said Haydee, noting that sometime before the incident in the shower, a fellow inmate had told Alex that he had been offered money to "take him out." Another inmate, she added, had also been extorting money from her son in exchange for not fabricating testimony against him.

"I think the time has come for us to get help," suggested Charlie as we drove back to Chicago. "From now on, things will only get worse, especially if they get new trials," he concluded.

After our visit, it became clear that we needed to approach the governor's office to ensure the safety of both Latinos. "Let's get a meeting with [Gov. Jim] Edgar or whoever oversees correctional institutions," suggested Pablo.

"That would be Howard Peters," said Meca. "I hear he's a pretty good guy."

After exchanging correspondence with the governor's office for more than a month, we heard from Illinois Department of Corrections Director Howard Peters. In a letter he assured us that Rolando "has not expressed any concerns relative to his safety or well-being" and that "Mr. Hernandez has been housed in the protective custody unit at Pontiac Correctional Center for quite some time."

Not happy with Peters' response, we decided to get the governor's attention one more time by holding him personally responsible for Alex's safety. Our strategy seemed to work. Days after we sent Edgar a second letter, Peter's office called to propose a meeting with the Coalition to discuss "housing options" for Alex.

Larry Marshall, who had asked to attend as an observer, warned us against meeting with Peters. "Remember he's already told you he can't move Alex due to the nature of the crime for which he was convicted."

"You, as an attorney, may have to take every 'yes' and every 'no' at face value," I reminded the Northwestern law professor. "We don't."

"Being an activist is all about changing people's minds," added Jean. "Sometimes it works, sometimes it doesn't, but it's still worth the try," she added cheerfully.

Despite the casual tone of Jean's remarks, every aspect of our meeting with the director of the Illinois Department of Corrections had been carefully planned. Miguel Jimenez, who represented a national organization that served the interests of Latinos with disabilities, had agreed to make the case for moving Alex out of Pontiac. "As you probably know, Mr. Peters, Alex is somewhat limited physically and emotionally, and consequently, unable to defend himself," he noted opening the meeting.

"Since Alex has been in prison, he has been beaten a number of times, and most recently, he's been told that he must pay $50 a week to an inmate or that the inmate will testify at his next trial and say that Alex confessed to him," added Tito.

"And there's also the latest incident involving another inmate who showed Alex a piece of paper with a phone number the inmate claims belongs to a former mayor of Naperville," I said. "According to Alex, this inmate has been offered money to kill him." I paused looking for the right words. "We can't wait to see if that happens, Mr. Peters. We believe Alex and Rolando will be vindicated and when that happens we expect to receive them back into the community alive. We're only asking you to provide a safe environment so they can survive their time in prison."

Charlie, for his part, stressed that the purpose for meeting with Peters was twofold. While we wanted Alex moved to another prison, he noted, we also wanted the head of the state's correctional system to understand that we would hold him and the governor personally responsible for the well being of both Latinos.

Our carefully crafted "the buck stops with you" strategy paid off. By the end of the meeting, Peters agreed to move Alex to the medium security Hill Correctional Center pursuant to his taking a polygraph test regarding the alleged hit on his life.

"Now that we made sure that Rolando and Alex are safe, why don't we try to convince Jim Ryan to do the right thing?" asked Sally filled with optimism.

"I believe Jim Ryan is worse than Burris," I told Sally. "He's not only responsible for prosecuting Rolando and

Alex but for doubting Cisowski's professional competence," I reminded her.

"Maybe now that he's going for statewide office, he'll want to consider the Latino organizations, elected officials and religious leaders that make up the Coalition for Justice," she countered.

"We could ask him if he plans to indict Dugan based on [Illinois Assistant Attorney General] Madsen's remarks at Rolando's Supreme Court hearing," suggested Charlie. "Now that I think about it, even one of Ryan's subordinates mentioned the possibility at either Rolando's or Alex' last trial. I'm sure it's on the record."

"Let's do it. We have nothing to lose," contended Tito.

With some Coalition members still leaning against the idea, on July 12, I requested to meet with the DuPage state's attorney in his role as Republican candidate for attorney general.

Over the phone, Ryan's assistant, Barbara Preiner, insisted that the meeting should be scheduled "on state's attorney's time." In an attempt to reach out to Ryan, we decided to put our request in writing. "We both know that this is an important issue you must face as you campaign for Illinois Attorney General, as the Chicago Sun Times Editorial Board refused to endorse you in the primary specifically due to the Nicarico case," we warned him in a letter dated the same day of my conversation with Preiner. "Therefore, your refusal to meet with us in Chicago as a candidate for attorney general should be reconsidered."

Far from reconsidering, Ryan wrote back insisting to meet in his office because the prosecution of Cruz and Hernandez involved the "execution of my official duties as DuPage County State's Attorney." On July 14, as we received Ryan's faxed response, we learned that the Illinois Supreme Court had reversed its 1992 decision and granted Rolando a new trial. Just hours after the ruling, in an impromptu press conference, Ryan announced he would retry Cruz for a third time. In response, we denounced Ryan's reaction to the high court as a political ploy.

"After initially contacting Jim Ryan, we are now declining his invitation to meet with him since he already publicly declared his position on the case," we said in a written statement. "We decry his duplicity for agreeing to meet with us to discuss Dugan's involvement in the Nicarico crime and hours later criticizing 'the media and others' for suggesting that Dugan should be tried for the murder. We believe our only recourse is to seek federal relief from the increasing and continuous violations of the civil rights of both Rolando Cruz and Alex Hernandez."

Ironically, as Jim Ryan embarked on yet another prosecutorial misadventure, Burris, in a smart final political move, declined to appeal the landmark Supreme Court decision that had won Rolando at least one more reprieve from the lethal injection.

CHAPTER VIII

The Federal Strategy

"To none will we sell, to none deny or delay, right or justice."
—The Magna Carta

ON JULY 18, 1994, representatives from the Coalition and Latino elected officials gathered in the lobby of the Thompson Center for a press conference to celebrate the Illinois Supreme Court decision granting Rolando a new trial. "Jim Ryan's handling of the Nicarico case has been impulsive and unprofessional, driven by personal ambition and political gain," I charged.

"He hasn't even taken time to review the Supreme Court ruling because his mind is already made up," added Jean, referring to Ryan's announcement to retry Rolando only five hours after the high court's decision had been made public.

"Even after Justice Charles E. Freeman stated that evidence about Dugan's other crimes could have 'bolstered Cruz's defense,' Ryan refuses to indict Dugan claiming he does not believe his confession," went on Tito. "Ryan's refusal, coupled with his unwillingness to grant Dugan immunity against the death penalty in exchange for his confession are nothing but a ploy to keep Cruz and Hernandez in an eternal legal limbo."

Our verbal attack on Ryan, far from being speculative, reflected the prosecutor's position on the Nicarico case. "While Ryan claims politics has nothing to do with his determination to keep Rolando behind bars, he suggests that the Justices' decision to grant Cruz another trial is the outcome of the change in the court's make up," I noted.

Ryan's remarks alluding to the politics of the Justices did not go unnoticed by the media either. The day after his pronouncement, several newspaper articles raised questions as to his own motivation for attacking the Supreme Court ruling. "Ryan, [however,] also pushed the political button a bit Thursday although he insisted that his jab was just a statement of fact," wrote the Chicago Tribune's Andrew Gottesman.

"Ryan – as November's Republican nominee for attorney general – and others high in [DuPage] County, are too politically and professionally vested in justifying past excesses, misrepresentations and egregious tactics to be ministers of the truth," contended the Tribune's Eric Zorn.

After publicizing our outrage about Ryan's pronouncement on Rolando, we turned our attention to Alex' appeal. Back in May of 1993, as the Illinois Supreme Court had decided to revisit Cruz's conviction, DuPage prosecutors and Alex' defense attorneys had agreed to put Hernandez's appeal on hold. Now that the ruling was out, Scott Turow and the team of attorneys who would be representing Alex had only days to ask the 2nd District Appellate Court in Elgin to grant their client a new trial.

"If I remember correctly, Alex was convicted merely on the basis of the testimony of a DuPage deputy who claimed he had overheard a conversation in Spanish, even though the deputy couldn't speak the language," said Tito as we reviewed the brief following the filing of the appeal.

According to the document, Alex had been placed in a police interrogation room with a childhood friend, Armindo Marquez, to help DuPage investigators solve an unrelated case where Marquez was the prime suspect. Later, the brief noted, a DuPage deputy sheriff had used the encounter to involve Alex in the Nicarico crime by saying that during his conversation with Marquez, Hernandez had made incriminating statements such as "I held the little girl down."

"The problem with this scenario is that, like the infamous girl's size 6 shoe, it doesn't fit," Pablo quipped. "First of all, part of the conversation between Alex and Marquez was in Spanish," he noted.

"Also, despite the importance of the alleged statement, Alex was not arrested for almost a year," I pointed out.

"Still, while testifying at Alex's trial more than a year later, the deputy recalled to the last detail Hernandez's part in the alleged conversation but could not remember anything that Marquez told Alex," added Tito.

"This is Rolando's 'vision' statement with a spin," proposed Maria.

"Worse," I insisted. "Here, DuPage investigators fooled Alex telling him he was helping solve a case."

"You're both right," stressed Sally. "First they tricked him and then, like they did with Rolando's alleged 'vision' statement, they didn't bother to record his words until a year later."

"And during all that time they didn't even arrest him," Tito reminded us.

"These tactics are the reason why we have to get the assistance of the U.S. Department of Justice," insisted Maria.

"It won't be easy," warned Charlie. "Before they agree to open an investigation, we'll have to convince them that the civil rights of Rolando and Alex were purposely violated by DuPage investigators and prosecutors."

Seeking federal relief for Cruz and Hernandez would definitely prove a difficult task. Our first setback came as we attempted to seek information from James B. Burns, the current U.S. Attorney for the Northern District of Illinois. "Present and past Assistant United States Attorneys employed by this office were directly involved in the initial prosecutions of Steven Buckley, Rolando Cruz and Alex Hernandez as Assistant DuPage County State's Attorneys. Therefore, the United States Attorney's office for this District will recuse itself from participating in any federal civil rights case arising from the prosecutions, in order to avoid even the appearance of conflict of interest," he wrote in response to our request.

Far from discouraging us, we took the U.S. attorney's recusal as a blessing in disguise. "After all, who wants prosecutors who have a lot to lose if there's a federal investigation involved in the process," noted Sally when we met to move forward with our initiative.

"That's right. We need to send our request straight to Washington, as far from Chicago, and, more importantly, as far from DuPage as possible," proposed Charlie.

"I can bring our request in person when I go to LULAC's convention in October," offered Maria who, as national vice-president, would be attending her organization's annual gathering.

"Before we send anything to Washington, we need to do a couple of things," cautioned Charlie. "First, we need to make sure everyone in the Illinois congressional delegation knows about our intentions, especially [U.S. Rep.] Luis Gutierrez. Then, we need to contact United Farm Workers President Arturo Rodriguez and Co-founder Dolores Huerta."

"Why not ask Luis to carry the ball," suggested Pablo. "After all, he's our highest elected official."

Tito agreed. "Let's meet with him and ask him to lead our efforts."

"I'll prepare a good package," proposed Efrain. Since the Coalition's inception, this quiet and behind-the-scenes kind of guy had been responsible for assembling every piece of media and legal information we needed to support our initiatives.

"Tomorrow is August 12th, and Rolando is going to be moved to DuPage County Jail," noted Jean. "Don't you think that at least we should make the Department of Justice aware of our concerns about his safety?"

"Absolutely, and we can also ask for their advice on how to initiate a request for a federal investigation. However, we shouldn't start it without getting the support of Luis [Gutierrez], Dolores [Huerta] and Artie [Rodriguez]," insisted Charlie.

"It makes sense. Luis knows the nuts and bolts of the federal government and the two leaders of the farm workers' movement have been using federal intervention as a strategy for years in their fight against racist and unscrupulous growers," agreed Pablo.

Before ending the meeting, each of us volunteered for an assignment. Sally and I would write the letter that Maria would take to the LULAC convention. Tito and Pablo would arrange the meeting with Luis Gutierrez and Sister Jean would make sure our concerns for Rolando's safety made it to the U. S. Department of Justice. As for Charlie, he would recruit the help of the Farm Workers' leadership to lobby for our efforts in Washington.

"At the time of our last meeting, only days before his death, Cesar [Chavez] and I discussed the Nicarico case and agreed that without Dugan's confession in a court of law, it will be difficult for Rolando and Alex to get justice," wrote Charlie in his letter to Dolores Huerta and Artie Rodriguez. "Due to the refusal of DuPage prosecutors to acknowledge Dugan as the sole perpetrator of this terrible crime, our only recourse at this time is to seek federal relief and ask the [U.S.] Department of Justice to protect both Latinos' civil rights. To make sure our request will have a favorable reception in Washington, we need your valuable help. These men's freedom will be a living tribute to Cesar's faith in their innocence," concluded Charlie.

While we pursued the federal strategy, Jim Ryan stepped up his efforts to retry Rolando by choosing the chief of the DuPage state's attorney's criminal division and a close friend, Joseph Birkett, to lead what Pablo referred to as a "prosecutorial witch hunt." According to media accounts, Birkett was next in line to replace Ryan if and when the state's attorney became Illinois attorney general.

"Politics rule," noted Sally as we discussed the appointment.

"It's obvious that this guy Birkett has an incentive to crucify Rolando," Tito mused.

"Besides politics, does DuPage have any other exports?" asked a sarcastic Maria.

"Death row inmates. After Cook [County], I believe DuPage is the county in the state with the most people on death row. But let's get back to the Feds," I proposed.

"Getting the attention of the Department of Justice remains a problem because the federal agency doesn't have jurisdiction to intervene in a case in progress," explained Charlie.

"Still, they should be made aware of our concerns for their safety and of our belief that their civil rights have been violated because unlike Buckley and Dugan, who are white, Rolando and Alex have been continually prosecuted despite the lack of physical evidence against them," stressed Jean.

Jean was right. At this point, everyone in the Coalition agreed that the two Latinos had not only been mistreated but also blatantly discriminated against by the DuPage criminal justice system. Now, we had to convince the federal government to step in.

"You should direct your request to [U.S. Senators] Paul Simon and Carol Moseley Braun, the Illinois Congressional delegation and the Hispanic Congressional Caucus," explained Luis Gutierrez as Tito, Pablo and I met in his Chicago office to discuss how to overcome the obstacles in our federal intervention strategy. "Also, whoever goes to Washington should hand-deliver copies of your request to the President and the Vice-president, to U.S. Attorney General Janet Reno and Deputy Attorney General John Schmidt, and most importantly, to Deval Patrick, the assistant attorney general in charge of the Civil Rights Division," he added, handing me a list. "Finally, address a letter with your request to me, have it signed by the state Latino elected officials who supported your resolution and I will deliver it personally to the Department of Justice," he concluded.

To reinforce the efforts of our congressman and the Farm Workers' leadership, we asked national Latino organizations like the Mexican American Legal Defense [MALDEF] and the National Council of La Raza (NCLR) to join us in making our case for federal intervention heard in Washington, D.C.

A few days after our discussion with Luis Gutierrez, Charlie received a phone call from UFW headquarters asking him to prepare a written plea for members of Congress who championed civil rights issues, like Senator Edward Kennedy. "While DuPage prosecutors chose not to retry Stephen Buckley after his first trial ended in a hung jury, they did not hesitate in retrying Alex Hernandez, a Latino whose second trial also ended in a hung jury," began Charlie expanding on Jean's rationale for seeking intervention. "While DuPage prosecutors refuse to indict Brian Dugan because they claim they have no proof against him, they insist on prosecuting Rolando Cruz, also a Latino, with flimsy evidence," he went on. "We are appealing to you because we believe you share our values and goals of ensuring the constitutional right of equal protection under the law for all people. Please, don't disappoint us," he concluded.

Meantime, while attending the national convention of the League of United Latin American Citizens, Maria succeeded in grabbing the attention of several prominent Washington residents. "At the executive committee meeting, when it was my turn to speak, I made the point that Cruz and Hernandez had been convicted for political reasons," she recalled, still energized by the experience. "I explained that Jim Ryan was now the Republican candidate for Illinois attorney general and therefore unwilling to admit that he had made a mistake letting Cruz sit on death row for ten years," Maria continued. "As I was finishing my presentation, I spotted [U.S. Associate Attorney General] John Schmidt standing in a corner, I waved for him to wait and handed him a package," she added like a quarterback who has just scored a touchdown.

"What about the resolution, did you get it passed?" asked Tito.

The measure, drafted by the Coalition on behalf of LULAC, called upon the members of Maria's organization "to make use of every medium at your disposal to correct the injustices perpetrated against Rolando Cruz and Alejandro Hernandez."

"It was unanimously approved," said Maria as she gave Tito a copy of the document.

"Were you able to talk to the President or the First Lady?" pressed Sally, eager for details on the political impact of Maria's trip.

"The evening of the banquet, I waited until Hillary [Rodham Clinton] had finished her speech and, after praising her oratory, I told her about the case and handed her another package," said Maria sporting a radiant smile.

"Should we start calling you the Federal Express lady?" kidded Pablo.

Maria quipped back. "In fact, that's what Janet Reno implied when I finished telling her that I had brought our request in person to make sure it didn't get lost in the mail. 'It's obvious you don't trust the post office,' she said."

"Well, Maria, if your trip doesn't do the trick, nothing will," I mused. "Now, let's get back to what we're doing here in Chicago. Our Latino elected officials are planning to endorse Al Hofeld for attorney general and they want our participation at the press conference," I announced.

"Didn't you meet with Hofeld and offer him some pointers?" joked Pablo.

"I did. But he claims he can't make Cruz and Hernandez the center of his campaign because, if elected attorney general, he might have to review their cases," I explained.

Fortunately, most of our elected officials did not face such constraints and on October 24, in an unprecedented display of solidarity, they came together to support Hofeld in his electoral bid.

"We call on voters to support Hofeld and question the record of his opponent, DuPage County State's Attorney Jim Ryan," read their joint press statement. "We have serious questions about the way Ryan's office has conducted the prosecution of Rolando Cruz and Alejandro Hernandez. Trigger-happy prosecutors care more about image than truth, place high profile convictions ahead of justice and put personal advancement before public accountability. We cannot afford this attitude in the office of the Attorney General," they charged.

"Our efforts paid off," whispered Maria as the press conference came to an end. "At least, the Latino leadership in Illinois is clear about their innocence."

Smiling back at Maria, I spotted Luis Gutierrez as he prepared to leave.

"I brought you the letter you requested, congressman," I said, rushing to Gutierrez.

"I need the signatures of the four state legislators who supported the resolution in Springfield," he reminded me.

As I collected the signatures of State Senators Miguel del Valle and Jesus Garcia and of State Reps. Ray Frias and Ben Martinez, I prayed that our concerted efforts would pay off.

Less than a month later, my prayers were answered, at least in part. Even though Jim Ryan won the November general election by a wide margin of votes, we received a written response from the U.S. Department of Justice acknowledging our request. In a letter dated December 2, 1994, Assistant Attorney General Deval L. Patrick instructed us to notify his office if we became aware of "evidence indicating that physical abuse has or will take place."

In his letter, Patrick also advised us to forward to his attention "any evidence that state prosecutors or any other law enforcement official intentionally used false evidence in order to secure the convictions of Mr. Hernandez and Mr. Cruz, so we can review those materials for potential violations of the federal criminal civil rights statutes."

Soon after, we celebrated yet another victory. Calling his conviction "fundamentally flawed," on January 30, 1995, the 2nd District Appellate Court ruled that Alex Hernandez would also receive a new trial.

CHAPTER IX

The Transfer

"Every sin is a result of a collaboration."
—Stephen Crane

FOLLOWING JIM RYAN's ascension to the Illinois attorney general's office, DuPage County Board Chairman Gayle Franzen appointed the county's chief judge, Anthony Peccarelli, to fill his vacancy. "Everybody's moving up, courtesy of Cruz and Hernandez," Efrain quipped as we met to review the status of our request for federal intervention. "Birkett, who's going to be the lead prosecutor at Rolando's next trial, is planning to run for Ryan's job and Robert Kilander, who forgot to tell defense attorneys that the shoe prints were a girl's size 6, is now a DuPage judge," he noted.

According to newspaper accounts, the professional success surrounding those involved in the prosecution of Cruz and Hernandez was not bound by county limits either. Patrick King, who had first heard about Dugan's confession but had kept it a secret from defense lawyers, was now an assistant U.S. attorney in the Chicago office. And Richard Stock, who had told jurors at Rolando's second trial that the [girl's size 6] shoe prints proved Cruz was guilty "beyond a reasonable doubt," had gone to work for his former boss, Jim Ryan, in the attorney general's office.

"They have all the prosecutorial bases covered, county, state and federal," noted Sally.

"So much for a system of checks and balances," retorted Charlie.

"That's why we need the Department of Justice on board," argued Pablo.

"When you say 'on board,' what exactly do you mean?" Efrain's question got everyone's attention. "We've already asked them for a federal prosecutor and they've said they don't have jurisdiction, so how much on board can they get?"

"According to Deval Patrick's letter, at least they can make sure Rolando and Alex are safe," offered Jean.

"That's true. The easiest way to make this case disappear would be to have Rolando and Alex get in trouble or worse," agreed Charlie. "Besides, once DuPage prosecutors find out that the Feds are on the lookout, they will start watching what they do and how they do it," he speculated.

"They'll think twice before putting a jailhouse snitch on the witness stand or pretending a girl's size 6 shoe belongs to Rolando. And if I were a DuPage sheriff's deputy, next time I'm called to testify I would consider claiming temporary amnesia," Tito mused.

"What's on the agenda for these guys?" asked Sally.

"Well, Rolando's trial is supposed to start soon. As for Alex, following in Jim Ryan's footsteps, Peccarelli has already announced he'll retry him but first he's asked the

Illinois Supreme Court to reverse the Illinois Appellate Court's decision. Ah, and like Jim Ryan, he'll refuse to plea-bargain with Dugan," I predicted.

"Let's face it. By refusing to plea bargain with Dugan, Jim Ryan has made sure that Alex and Rolando remain in a legal limbo," reflected Jean. "When you have jurors admitting that if they had heard all the evidence about Dugan they would have found Rolando and Alex innocent, you realize that unless that happens there's little hope they'll ever be cleared of this terrible crime."

"Even if all of Dugan's evidence comes out, Rolando and Alex won't be exonerated as long as the DuPage criminal justice system keeps on treating them as Dugan's accomplices," I noted.

"The Dugan 'et al' theory," added Charlie, "has two major flaws. The first one is that according to Cisowski's investigation, almost 80 people said that Dugan did not know either Cruz or Hernandez."

"This makes a conspiracy among thieves improbable. After all, how many strangers team up to commit a crime?" Tito joked.

"The second problem with trying to pair Dugan with Cruz and Hernandez, is that according to experts, pedophiles usually act alone," Maria pointed out.

"Still, I doubt that without Dugan's confession, Rolando and Alex can ever be fully exonerated," predicted Pablo.

"Even if they have a bench trial?" asked Efrain.

"Well, just look at the judges who presided over the past trials. Most of them granted every motion to the prosecution, including keeping Dugan's other crimes and his DNA away from the jurors," argued Pablo.

"We'll see what Rolando's new judge, Ronald Mehling, does with the latest motion from Cruz's attorneys. They want prosecutors to reveal whether Rolando committed the murder with Hernandez and Buckley, as they claimed at his first trial, or with Alex and Dugan, as they argued at his second trial," I noted.

"They'll have to go with Dugan. Buckley has already sued them for misconduct," retorted Sally. "What I would like to know, related to the same motion, is where they're going to say the murder took place."

Sally's curiosity was well justified. At Cruz's first trial, prosecutors had supported the theory that Jeanine had been killed near the Illinois Prairie Path. At Cruz's second trial, after Dugan had admitted killing Jeanine at the Path, prosecutors contended that she had been murdered elsewhere.

"There's another interesting point in this motion related to the weapon used to commit the murder," I noted. "At Cruz's second trial, prosecutors said it was most likely a baseball bat. But at Alex's second trial they claimed it was a lead-filled billy club. If I'm not mistaken, an old acquaintance of Dugan's who was interviewed by the state police said that Dugan always carried a club under the front seat of his car," I added.

"I wonder what prosecutors will do if this time DNA results prove that only Dugan could have committed the rape," said Jean, noting that Judge Mehling had already authorized the new testing. "I heard that it's far more precise now than it was in 1989."

"Forget the DNA," rebuffed Pablo. "They'll claim that even if Dugan raped Jeanine Nicarico, Rolando and Alex still killed her."

"It won't be that easy," I warned Pablo. "Remember the many witnesses who said that Dugan, Cruz and Hernandez didn't know each other," I reminded him.

"But if Dugan's genetic sample matches the semen found in Jeanine Nicarico, DuPage prosecutors at least have to charge him with rape," protested Efrain.

"The problem is that nobody seems to give a damn about Dugan. As far as the DuPage criminal justice system is concerned, he doesn't even exist," retorted Tito.

"That's exactly what gets me, that nobody in DuPage gives a damn about Dugan," blurted Pablo. "If instead of Rolando and Alex, two nice boys from Naperville had gotten into this mess, I'm sure they wouldn't have ended up in prison just for hustling a ten thousand-dollar reward, or, like in Alex' case, for trying to help solve a crime," he challenged.

"You're right, Pablo. Your 'two nice boys from Naperville' would have enjoyed white privilege their whole lives," said Jean. "No policeman would have taken them in for questioning without their parents or their lawyer. They would have never *de facto* been considered a threat, and, most importantly, they would have never been regarded expendable. On the other hand, two Latinos from Aurora with no jobs and a couple of minor run-ins with the law make the perfect suspects when time is running out and political expediency takes precedence over truth," added Jean sorrowfully.

"That's why it's so important to keep on promoting these guys' innocence," I reminded everyone. "Every time people hear us talk about the case, at least they wonder why, and that's good."

"You're right. Many people have asked me why I'm trying so hard to get these guys out of prison, especially because like Sally, I'm not exactly a bleeding heart liberal," joked Maria, noting that she had recently been appointed to a state university board by "our very Republican" Governor Jim Edgar.

"Didn't you recently give a talk about the case? How did it go?" asked Jean looking in my direction.

"It was last month, on March 8, at a journalism work-shop organized by Columbia College. Besides discussing the case, I talked about the role of the media – particularly the Spanish-language media – in helping us promote our initiatives. As an example, I told them about our trip to Springfield and how Channel 44, despite having only two mobile units, sent a camera crew to cover the whole-day-event," I recalled.

"By the way, Diana and I are planning to visit Alex at Hill Correctional Center in Galesburg to find out how he's doing now that he's in the medium security prison," announced Charlie.

"Didn't you also send a letter to the governor asking him to keep Alex at Hill throughout his next trial?" asked

Sally, aware that like Rolando, Alex would soon be moved to the DuPage jail where we believed he had been tricked into becoming a suspect.

"Before communicating further with the governor's office or with the Department of Justice, I think we should wait until we come back from Galesburg," I replied.

On April 19, Charlie and I walked into the medium security facility where Alex had been staying for almost a year.

"It looks like a school cafeteria," said Haydee as she escorted us into the prison's visiting room.

After a short wait, Alex walked in accompanied by a correctional officer. As soon as we shook hands, I noticed that the young Puerto Rican was exactly as I had pictured him – a gentle individual whose minor youthful indiscretions in no way justified the ordeal he was suffering at the hands of the DuPage criminal justice system.

After we had our picture taken by another correctional officer "armed" with a Polaroid, Alex pointed us in the direction of a patio. "Let's go out there," he said. "I have something to tell you and we'll have more privacy."

Intrigued, I pointed to an empty outdoor table. "We can sit right here."

"I don't want to ruin your visit," started Alex after he made sure nobody was around. "But my mom says you want me to speak out if I'm worried about my safety, right?"

"Of course," replied Charlie.

Alex seemed unsure of what to say next. "The last time I was in DuPage jail, I got sick," he uttered almost in a whisper. "If they take me back there, I'll be afraid to drink or eat anything they give me."

"Would you be willing to take a lie detector test about what you just said, like the one you took about the threats at Pontiac?" asked Charlie.

"Yes, but there's something else," he added.

Perceiving the apprehension in her son's eyes, Haydee took over the conversation. "Do you remember the DuPage deputy sheriff who worked in the jail and said that Alex broke down and admitted going to the Nicarico's to do a robbery?" she asked.

"Wasn't he the same guy who said nothing about the statement until almost four years later?" Suddenly, it hit me. If Haydee and I were talking about the same individual, he could attempt to frame Alex like he had done once before.

"I heard that he's now in charge of transferring inmates from the state prisons to the DuPage jail," resumed Haydee.

"Well, we'll have to find a way to keep him away from Alex," I said.

"Don't worry, he'll be safe," Charlie reassured Haydee as we prepared to leave.

"One last thing," remembered Alex. "I got a letter from Dan Webb, the attorney. He says he wants to represent me at my next trial."

"That's great news," I cheered. Unfortunately, my enthusiasm was short-lived.

In the letter, went on Alex, Webb admitted being a friend and a supporter of Jim Ryan, the man we believed was responsible for keeping him behind bars for more than ten years.

As soon as we returned from Galesburg, we met to discuss Webb's offer.

"We don't know if they're still friends," warned Pablo in an attempt to downplay the issue. "This case has turned many lawyers against each other. Gary Johnson, for example, before defending Steven Buckley, was also Ryan's pal. But in a letter to the judge who presided over Alex' third trial, he openly criticized Ryan's handling of the case, going as far as to compare the Cruz and Hernandez saga to the Rodney King scandal," he noted.

"As you said, Gary Johnson used to be a friend of Jim Ryan," I said, underscoring the term 'used to'. "In Webb's case, though, they're still friends. And if what Haydee told me is right, Webb was Ryan's campaign chairman when he ran for attorney general," I cautioned.

"As everyone knows, it is the campaign chairman's duty to publicly praise a candidate's performance, which in Jim Ryan's case would include his handling of the Nicarico prosecution," added Charlie.

Judging from Webb's letter, a copy of which I had gotten from Alex himself, it was hard to assess the degree of his friendship with Jim Ryan. While Webb acknowledged in writing that "former DuPage County State's Attorney Jim Ryan is a personal friend of mine and I have supported him in his political career," the former federal prosecutor also wrote that he was "excited" at the prospect of representing Alex so he would be able to "put this matter behind you once and for all." The only way to clarify the situation, we agreed, would be to meet personally with Webb and openly discuss our concerns.

The meeting took place a few weeks later at the penthouse conference room of Winston & Strawn, the prestigious legal firm where Webb was a senior partner. Flanked by his associates, the prominent attorney spoke candidly of his ties to Jim Ryan, but restated his commitment to Alex.

"Do you think Webb will honestly try to clear Alex' name or will he merely bargain for his freedom without muddying the waters for his good friend, Jim Ryan?" asked Sally after the meeting.

"There's no easy answer for your question. After all, it is common practice for a defense attorney to cut a deal with the prosecution," noted Jean.

"As long as Webb succeeds in getting Alex out we have no right to object to his involvement," warned Charlie.

"I agree. After all, in order to clear his name, Alex needs to be free," acknowledged Pablo.

"Right now, we should deal with his safety if he's forced to return to DuPage. Especially if the transfer is handled by the DuPage sheriff's office," added Sally.

"Can't Webb get the judge to move Alex to another jail?" asked Maria.

"He can and he will," I replied. "But he must wait until the actual transfer takes place. What we, as advocates, need to do, is to make sure that someone from the Illinois Department of Corrections, and not from the DuPage sheriff's office, takes Alex from Galesburg to DuPage," I explained.

"So I assume that the Illinois Department of Corrections can't keep Alex at Hill throughout his trial," ventured Tito.

"That's correct. IDOC's jurisdiction will cease as soon as they receive written notification that Alex' conviction has been reversed," I explained.

"Then, we should ask the U.S. Department of Justice to intervene based on their instructions about safety," proposed Pablo.

It was agreed. While Webb dealt with Alex' transfer in the courts, we would have the federal agency reinforce Webb's efforts by sending a warning to the DuPage sheriff's office.

In the weeks that followed, as we met again to formalize our request, we learned that DuPage Judge Roland Mehling had granted a postponement on Rolando's trial.

"According to this article, Birkett has to be replaced because he's the lead prosecutor in the trial of a Naperville stockbroker accused of stabbing his former wife to death," said Efrain reading from a newspaper.

"It looks like they're trying to prop him up for the next DuPage state's attorney primary," mused Sally, who believed the switch was a political move to keep Birkett out of the controversy that would surround Cruz's next trial.

"The only thing we can do is notify the Feds of the delay and ask them to monitor Rolando while he's in the DuPage jail," suggested Jean.

"By the way, how is Alex's transfer coming along?" interrupted Maria, visibly worried.

"The Illinois Department of Corrections has agreed to transport Alex to DuPage instead of having [DuPage County Sheriff] Doria's people pick him up at Hill. As for the Department of Justice, I've prepared a letter asking them to bring our concerns directly to Doria," I said.

"That won't hurt Rolando either," Pablo mused.

"Are you sure the Department of Justice will tell Doria to transfer Alex out of DuPage?" asked Tito,

"Let's wait and see," I replied.

Days later, I addressed our request to Deval Patrick, the chief of the criminal section at the department's division of civil rights. "We are aware of all the jurisdictional limitations that seem to prevent state and federal authorities from conducting a thorough investigation on a county jail system that we fear has been at best irresponsible in their treatment of Mr. Hernandez and Mr. Cruz. However, we know it is our right and duty to state our fears for the record," I wrote.

On June 7, officers from the Illinois Department of Correction drove Alex to the DuPage Jail. "Well, at least the governor did his share," noted Maria as I called her to break the news. "Now let's hope the transfer comes through," she added before we hung up.

Our concerted efforts paid off. On June 11, Webb pleaded for his client's safety with DuPage Judge Thomas Callum, who had been appointed to preside over Hernandez's next trial. The following day Alex was quietly transferred to nearby Kendall County Jail.

Ironically, we learned that the U.S. Department of Justice had played a key role in the transfer thanks to Doria's own admissions to the media. According to the DuPage sheriff, an agent representing the Federal Bureau of Investigations had warned him that if authorities received further complaints against his office, they would launch a full civil rights investigation.

"We haven't had a civil rights complaint about our facility in more than ten years, and I want to keep it that way," he was quoted as saying. "If he wants out of DuPage, I'll be happy to get him out. We don't want any trouble from him."

"Finally, the wheels of justice are turning for Cruz and Hernandez," proclaimed Tito as we toasted the transfer.

"I have a feeling that soon Alex and Rolando will see the light of freedom," predicted Jean.

As Cesar Chavez had once said: "Truth gets better with time." For the first time since the Coalition had become involved in this case, I was starting to understand why.

CHAPTER X

Cruz and Hernandez Freed

"Truth gets better with time."

—Cesar Chavez

IN THE WEEKS THAT FOLLOWED Alex' transfer to Kendall County, we discussed our next course of action. "Rolando's trial is set to start on October 24. I think we should use the tape," I said referring to a videotaped confession of Dugan I had received anonymously in the mail.

"Let's have a community forum and share the confession with our leaders and organizations. I'm sure they'll find the tape revealing, to say the least," Tito mused.

"Revealing? Shocking would be better. As a mother and a grandmother, I can't tell you how I felt the first time I saw Dugan describe the rape and murder as if he was describing an outing," said Maria, lending a personal touch to Tito's point.

"Let's watch it one more time so we can decide what part we want to edit," proposed Efrain as he rewound the tape to the point where a hypnotized Dugan recalled how he had killed the Naperville girl.

"There," cried out Tito, closely following the printed version of Dugan's videotaped confession. "I think we should publicize this part in case prosecutors push the theory that Dugan is responsible for the rape but that Cruz and Hernandez committed the murder."

Dugan's account of how he had bludgeoned Jeanine Nicarico to death exceeded the most gruesome expectations. "I told her that I was going to take her back home, that she'd have to get into the front seat of the car, and I opened the door, and we walked around the back of the car and I hit her with the tire iron, twice. She fell and hit her head on my bumper, and I hit her again. I grabbed her by her nightgown and dragged her into the trees and I let go of her, and I hit her again with a board, a piece of tree limb that didn't have any bark on it."

"It's unbelievable that after viewing this tape and after Cisowski's conclusion about Dugan, Jim Ryan persisted in trying Rolando and Alex," I said almost in a whisper.

"And don't forget the lie detector test," added Charlie.

"Do we have a copy? Maybe we should also make it public," suggested Maria.

"Here it is," said Efrain, flaunting the transcript of the testimony of polygraph examiner Thomas Walsh.

"According to this guy, before submitting to the test, Dugan discussed the murder in detail. This is important, because if I'm not mistaken, DuPage prosecutors dismissed the test results saying that, besides answering 'yes' or 'no' to Walsh's questions, Dugan did not make any statements about the Nicarico crime," I noted.

"Still, while undergoing the procedure, according to this transcript, Dugan admitted kicking in the door of the Nicarico home, killing Jeanine, not making up the story about the killing, being alone when he committed the rape and the murder, and not making up the confession to get Cruz, Buckley or Hernandez off the hook," said Efrain reading from the document. "Isn't that enough?"

"Unfortunately, lie detector tests are inadmissible in court," warned Jean.

"I don't care. To tear down the walls that keep Dugan off this case, we must enter both, the videotaped confession and the lie detector test as evidence in the court of public opinion. Let the people decide," proposed Maria.

"I agree. Besides, unless 'we the people' find a way to expose Dugan for the Nicarico crime, Cruz and Hernandez will never be exonerated," I predicted.

"Are you telling me that DuPage will never charge Brian Dugan, even if his DNA matches the semen found in the Naperville girl?" asked Efrain taken by surprise.

"Jim Ryan and his successors have consistently denied Dugan's involvement in the Nicarico case because the state's attorney's office overlooked the fact that long before Jeanine, he had already raped and kidnapped other children in DuPage and in Kane County," Jean reminded us.

"What I don't understand is why Jim Ryan dismissed Cisowski's investigation and even accused the state police commander of feeding information to Dugan to make him look guilty of the Nicarico murder," protested Maria.

"There's something else we're forgetting," I cautioned. "If Jim Ryan, or his successors, had agreed to plea bargain with Dugan, everyone who had anything to do with, should I say, enhancing the evidence against Rolando, Alex and Buckley, would be irremissibly exposed."

"Which is exactly what a federal investigation will do," observed Sally. "If we agree that the DuPage criminal justice system is so entangled in a web of deceit that it will never recognize Dugan as the murderer of Jeanine Nicarico, then, we better ask the Feds to step in," she reasoned.

"I think we should attack from different fronts," said Pablo, speaking like a general preparing for war. "On one front, we should have a community forum so we can discuss Dugan. On another front, we should have a letter campaign insisting that DuPage should indict Dugan. And on a third front, we have to reinforce our request for federal intervention with a more aggressive initiative, maybe with a petition drive to U.S. Attorney General Janet Reno."

"The quality of the tape needs to be improved," I noted. "Let me call a few people and find out what can be done."

"Meanwhile, I'll write the draft letter to [acting DuPage State's Attorney Anthony] Peccarelli," offered Jean.

"I'll get the University of Illinois at Chicago to host the event," offered Maria, who shared a close relationship with the college president.

"I'll deal with the refreshments and the press releases," volunteered Sally.

"And I'll take care of the information packages," promised Efrain.

"One more thing, we need to decide when to have the event," said Pablo looking at a huge calendar across the room.

"A few days before Rolando's trial and as close as possible to Columbus Day," suggested Maria, noting that the holiday commemorated the closing of Hispanic Heritage Month.

"This year, it falls on Monday, October 9. Let's have the forum that day, so everyone can make it," proposed Pablo.

"As soon as Maria finds out if the day is O.K. with U. of I., Efrain and I will take care of the invitations," added Tito.

While organizing the three different strategies was complicated and time consuming, editing Dugan's confession proved to be almost impossible. After reviewing the tape at the headquarters of *La Raza* and at the sound department of Columbia College, two experts agreed that the only way it would be of any use was if Dugan's words were incorporated into the video through a process called sub-titling.

"It was quite an expensive process," I explained as we gathered to put the final touches on the October 9th event. "Fortunately, in a display of solidarity, Jose Francisco and Armando agreed to have it done at the station," I noted.

"Are you telling me that Don Jose Francisco Lamas, general manager of Channel 44-Telemundo, and his second in command, Dr. Armando Triana, both outstanding members of the Cuban American community, are openly supporting a cause against the DuPage criminal justice system?" quipped Tito.

"Channel 44 has always been there for us, whether it was at a press conference in Chicago or at a march in Springfield," replied Sally. "Besides, Cuban Americans, like any other Latinos, despise abuse of power."

"Sally's right," agreed Jean. "I think that we should feel very proud that most of the Latino leaders have put aside ideology and even nationalism to support this case."

"Going back to the forum, do we want the media to attend the whole event or do we want them at a press conference afterwards?" asked Efrain.

"I propose we first have the forum and then the press conference," suggested Pablo.

"How many copies of the tape should we have available for the media?" asked Sally.

"One for each TV station, plus a copy for major newspapers and the news radio stations. And don't worry about making too many copies. They'll all come," predicted Charlie.

"I agree. By the way, at the forum we should also discuss the new DNA test results because they not only exclude Rolando but point at Dugan as the alleged rapist of Jeanine Nicarico," I noted. As reported by the Chicago Tribune, this time experts had found that Dugan's DNA matched the genetic material in the sperm found in Jeanine's body and that "this particular DNA is shared by only 0.03 percent of the male Caucasian population."

"So we can safely assume that Dugan was Jeanine's rapist," exclaimed Efrain.

"Which unfortunately doesn't get Rolando and Alex off the hook," cautioned Sally. "This time, DuPage prosecutors will claim that even if Dugan may have been involved, Cruz and Hernandez were with him."

"Let me see. Cruz, Hernandez and Dugan went to do a burglary together but changed their minds and decided to kidnap, rape and murder Jeanine Nicarico," started out Pablo, making light of the prosecution's theory. "Then, after Cruz and Hernandez were arrested, they spoke about their own involvement in the crime but never mentioned Dugan, not even to try to lessen their own sentences."

"And not even after Dugan confessed," added Charlie sarcastically.

"Remember that there are at least two holes in that theory," I countered. "The first one is that so far nobody has been able to prove Dugan knew Cruz or Hernandez, much less that they committed a crime together," I pointed out.

The second hole in their "multiple intruders" theory, I explained, had been recently unearthed in one of Eric Zorn's informative columns about the case. "For the first time, I've learned that [former Naperville Police Chief] James Teal and [former DuPage Detective] John Sam, knew from the beginning that the investigation focused on 'a single individual, possibly a sex offender, age 25-35, known to kick in doors in burglaries, drive a green sedan, and who had perhaps skipped work on the day of the murder,'" wrote Zorn.

"If that's true, why did DuPage even bother to bring charges against two Latinos who had no history of committing sexual crimes?" asked a perplexed Pablo.

"This confirms what we've been saying all along. They didn't do their job. Otherwise Dugan would have been caught before he had a chance to murder Donna Schnorr and Melissa Ackerman," charged Maria. "That's why we need to move forward with the federal investigation."

"And that's why we need to show Dugan's confession to the world," concluded Pablo.

On October 9, 1995, more than 50 community and political leaders came to the University of Illinois at Chicago to discuss the speculations and rhetoric of a criminal justice system that seemed more interested in keeping Cruz and Hernandez behind bars than in finding the real killer of Jeanine Nicarico.

Following the screening of the videotaped confession, our leaders expressed their concerns about Rolando's upcoming trial. "It's time for Dugan to be indicted," noted one elected official.

As our community forum came to a close, TV cameras and reporters overflowed the room. "Let us always keep in mind, that in an effort to achieve a crime-free society, we should not allow ourselves to violate the rights of individuals regardless of their race or ethnicity – a principle integral to the criminal justice system of any civilized nation," read our press statement.

"We don't want another trial, the community doesn't want another trial. We want Cruz and Hernandez freed and Dugan indicted. Whether they have to plea bargain with him or not, we don't care," I told reporters.

Our press conference received extensive coverage. As a bonus, prominent newscaster Bill Kurtis introduced our segment telling WBBM Channel 2 viewers, that "Latino community groups say enough is enough." Another renowned journalist and Kurtis' former partner, WFLD's Walter Jacobson, emphasized that "[the Coalition] wants a grant of immunity [from the death penalty] to be given to Brian Dugan. That, says the Coalition, is the only way to clear suspects Rolando Cruz and Alejandro Hernandez."

Despite our success in getting our message across and the continuous airing of Dugan's videotaped confession, Rolando's third trial started as scheduled, on October 24. According to Jean, who attended the trial, DuPage County Assistant State's Attorney John Kinsella, who had replaced Joe Birkett as the lead prosecutor, devoted much of his opening remarks to dispute Dugan's claims.

As expected, the prosecution's cornerstone was the so called "vision" statement. "[DuPage sheriff deputies] Vosburgh and Kurzawa were totally focused. They didn't even blink," noted Jean as she recounted their testimony.

"If they keep on putting credible people on the stand, it will be hard for defense attorneys to prove Rolando's innocence," predicted Tito when we met to discuss the status of our petition drive to Janet Reno.

"Besides more than 50 organizations, we have plenty of signatures from prominent religious and political leaders," I announced at the meeting. Among the individuals urging the U.S. attorney general to open a civil rights investigation, I noted, were Monsignor Ken Velo, Cardinal Joseph Bernardin's secretary and confidant, Luis Gutierrez, Illinois' first and only Latino U.S. congressman, and Dolores Huerta and Artie Rodriguez, the leaders of the United Farm Workers' Union. "We'll have the petitions on Reno's desk by October 30, which is next Monday," I promised the group.

Our timing could not have been better. On the same week we flooded the U.S. attorney general's office with the signatures of numerous local and national leaders, Judge Mehling dismissed the case against Rolando.

"It was fast," recalled Jean. "When DuPage Lieutenant Robert Montesano was called to the stand, the prosecutor asked him if officers Vosburgh and Kurzawa had called his home to report that Rolando had told them about the vision."

"And all of a sudden, we heard Montesano say 'No, I don't recall that,'" interrupted Tito. "It was awesome because, as we later found out, the guy had said just the opposite at a pre-trial deposition only a few months earlier."

"After a moment of stunned silence," continued Jean, "the prosecution asked for a recess but the defense objected because they wanted to cross examine Montesano. So Mehling sided with Rolando's lawyers and Montesano was asked to explain why he had changed his mind," Jean went on.

"According to Montesano," Tito said as if he were throwing a fastball, "his wife had recently found some credit cards receipts that proved he was on vacation in Florida when he was supposed to have received the phone call from Vosbourgh and Kurzawa."

"Why would Montesano suddenly incriminate himself and his subordinates for some stupid receipts," asked Maria, "unless he was afraid that someone had copies?"

"Like the Feds," blurted Pablo.

"I agree. Otherwise, he could have done what Haydee said the DuPage prosecutor did when she gave him the receipt that proved Alex was in a store in another town at the time of the murder," mused Tito.

"Do you think our petitions did the trick?" asked an ebullient Efrain.

"I don't know but it's ironic that the demise of the prosecution's case was caused by the same 'vision' statement that DuPage thought was their best piece of evidence against Rolando," noted Sally.

"And most of what we sent to the Department of Justice had to do with that statement," added Efrain fueling his speculation that Montesano's change of heart was somewhat linked to our request for a federal investigation.

"Truth gets better with time," Charlie reminded us. "Soon, it will be Alex's turn."

Charlie's prediction was right on target. On November 20, less than a week after Rolando's release, I stood in a packed courtroom holding Haydee's hand as Judge Callum freed Alex on a $400,000 bond – $45,000 less than what his defense attorney, Dan Webb, had requested.

Two days later, the U.S. Department of Justice agreed "to have the FBI conduct an investigation into the allegations that certain law enforcement officers may have fabricated evidence in an attempt to deprive Mr. Cruz of his right to a fair trial."

And on December 8, in what we thought was an attempt to save face, the DuPage County state's attorney's office dropped all charges against Alex.

Still, our quest for justice was far from over. In the years to come, not only would the DuPage criminal justice system fail to apologize for the unjust prosecutions of both Latinos, but would continue to ignore Dugan as a viable suspect despite the incriminating DNA that directly linked him to the rape and murder of Jeanine Nicarico.

Till Justice is Done

"JUSTICE WON'T BE DONE until Brian Dugan is charged and Jim Ryan and others admit that, at best, they made a mistake prosecuting – and persecuting – Cruz and Hernandez for more than ten years," I warned viewers during the first January 1996 segment of "*Mesa Redonda*."

"Only the indictment of Brian Dugan will bring true vindication for Rolando and Alex and hopefully, final resolution for the Nicarico family," agreed Maria, concerned about Jeanine's parents steadfast repudiation of the two Latinos, even after their release from prison.

"Those who overstepped the mandate of a fair and proper criminal justice system in exchange for political gain will some day have to answer to a higher power, here on earth or in the after life," predicted state Sen. Jesus "Chuy" Garcia as he discussed the political overtones of the case. "It is indisputable that personal ambition played a key role in the indictment and prosecution of the two Latinos. I exhort those responsible to come forward and admit they were at best misguided in relying on evidence that wasn't there while at the same time ignoring the overwhelming evidence against Dugan."

Far from acknowledging any mistakes during his involvement in the case, Jim Ryan insisted that he had acted properly "given the state of admissible evidence." As for his successor, Anthony Peccarelli, in the aftermath of Cruz's third trial, he asked DuPage County Chief Judge Edward Kowal to appoint a special prosecutor to scrutinize allegations of wrongdoing.

"This initiative is just a ploy to undermine our request for a federal investigation," charged Pablo during an interview following the appointment. "First, Kowal is the same judge who sentenced Rolando to death, not once but twice, despite the conflicting evidence at both trials," he noted. "Second, he has appointed William J. Kunkle, Jr., a well-known law and order attorney and a friend of Jim Ryan, to conduct the investigation."

Subsequent media accounts supported Pablo's remarks. "In appointing him [Kunkle], DuPage Chief Judge Edward Kowal has all but guaranteed that the independent investigation into the Cruz case will create controversy rather than quell it," speculated Eric Zorn in his weekly column following the appointment.

"I think this [Kunkle's appointment] underscores the fact that we need an independent investigation by the Justice Department or someone like that, not a prosecutor who is appointed by the judge who twice sentenced Cruz to the death penalty," said G. Flynt Taylor during an interview with the Chicago Sun-Times.

Despite the criticism, in December of 1996, a DuPage grand jury returned a 47-count indictment against three former county prosecutors and four current sheriff's deputies who had been involved in the Nicarico case.

Days before the indictments of the men who for the next three years would be known as the "DuPage seven," Cruz and Hernandez also filed lawsuits alleging that the DuPage criminal justice system had conspired to fabricate evidence against them while concealing other evidence that would have exonerated them.

"Conspiring is the key word," noted Tito, as members of the Coalition got together to review the year's progress by the U.S. Department of Justice.

"Have you heard anything new?" asked Jean, who like Pablo, was concerned that the DuPage initiative would dilute the federal investigation.

"Last March, I received a second and last letter from [U.S. Assistant Attorney General] Deval Patrick confirming that if there is a prosecutable violation of federal criminal civil rights statutes, they will act appropriately," I said. "However, I have a feeling they won't do anything until this circus in DuPage is over."

"Actually, after reading about the indictments, I'm even more sure that the DuPage Circus, as you call it, was conceived to stop the federal investigation," insisted Pablo.

"Pablo's right. If not, how come Jim Ryan and Sheriff Doria were not included?" asked Tito.

Echoing Tito's claims, as the probe ended, the editorial board of the Chicago Tribune questioned Kunkle's decision to limit the indictments to the "DuPage Seven." "And what of those not indicted but also, in some way, implicated in the wrongful prosecution of Rolando Cruz. What, especially of Atty. Gen. Jim Ryan, who as DuPage state's attorney authorized two separate prosecutions of Cruz?"

As for the DuPage sheriff, while he was not indicted, neither did he elude the barbs of the Tribune's Eric Zorn. When in March of 1997, Gov. Edgar nominated the recently retired Doria to the Illinois Prisoner Review Board, Zorn charged that "at virtually every other funky turn along the way – the so-called vision statement, reports not written, leads ignored, testimony that changes oddly – one finds direct involvement by officers under Doria, who continues to back their actions 100 percent."

In a predictable turn of events, almost three years and more than $3 million after the indictments, DuPage County Sheriff's detectives Thomas Vosburgh and Dennis Kurzawa, Lieutenants Robert Winkler and James Montesano, and former Assistant State's Attorneys Thomas Knight, Patrick King and Robert Kilander were exonerated in a DuPage courtroom. According to media accounts, the jurors who acquitted them celebrated their vindication by attending a party in their honor.

"Imagine having the jurors who absolved you from a crime celebrate with you. Only in DuPage!" Efrain mused as we discussed the outcome of the trial.

"It's another mockery of the criminal justice process," charged Tito.

As for the lawsuits filed by Buckley, Cruz and Hernandez, in September of 2000, the DuPage County Board settled them. The terms of the settlement, I thought, were appalling. Not only were Cruz, Hernandez and Buckley forced to accept a mere $3.5 million – much less than the $100 million their attorneys claimed the case was worth – but they were subjected to the ridicule and scorn of DuPage county board members who called the settlement "go away money" and a "business decision" aimed at saving millions more in litigation costs. And to top it all, there was the "we would bring them down into the basement and shoot them," comment, which went grossly under-reported and minimally criticized, even by those who pride themselves as zealous guardians of political correctness.

"What I can't understand is why DuPage still refuses to indict Dugan," complained Sally weeks after the settlement, as we got together to decide if there was anything else that we should do to help justice prevail in this convoluted and still unresolved murder case.

"Don't you people get it?" challenged Pablo. "As long as Dugan remains in the dark, DuPage public officials can go on saying that Cruz, Hernandez and Buckley were 'somewhat' involved in the Nicarico crime."

"And what's more important, Jim Ryan and others can keep on running for office free of Brian Dugan's shadow," added Maria.

"Are you suggesting that despite the new DNA, current DuPage State's Attorney Joe Birkett will never charge Dugan?" asked Tito visibly upset.

To this day, he has not. Meanwhile, Brian Dugan remains in an Illinois prison, where he is serving two life terms for raping and killing Donna Schnorr and Melissa

Ackerman. But as long as he is not indicted for the murder of Jeanine Nicarico, justice will not be done.

Afterword 2013

As this book was printed, Jim Ryan and Joseph Birkett, who continued to insist that Rolando Cruz and Alex Hernandez "may have been implicated in the Nicarico crimes," even after the two Latinos had been legally exonerated and compensated for their wrongful imprisonment, chose to run for governor and attorney general of the state of Illinois.

Thanks to the assistance of United Farm Workers Co-founder Dolores Huerta, who secured Diana Eiranova-Kyle a grant from the Vanguard Foundation to write and produce a documentary about the Coalition for Justice's involvement in the case, the coalition—armed with this book and with the documentary—was able to expose the DuPage prosecutors' misleading assertions, including Birkett's refusal to indict Brian Dugan alleging that the DNA evidence against him was insufficient despite a public campaign that the coalition had kicked off in 2001 asking the prosecutor, as DuPage County State's Attorney, to plea bargain with the convicted serial killer so he would publicly confess to the Nicarico crimes. In great part due to their involvement in the wrongful prosecutions of Rolando Cruz and Alex Hernandez, in their denials that they had done anything wrong, and in Birkett's refusal to indict Dugan despite the overwhelming DNA evidence against him, Jim Ryan and Joseph Birkett lost their political races.

Between 2002 and 2009, the Coalition for Justice continued to pressure Birkett to indict Brian Dugan for the Nicarico crimes. In 2009, after suffering another political defeat in 2006 when he attempted a run for the lieutenant governor's office, unable to argue against the overwhelming DNA evidence that he had dismissed for so long, Birkett finally indicted Brian Dugan but instead of plea bargaining with the convicted killer to save taxpayers money—which had already been wasted in countless legal battles to put Cruz and Hernandez to death—the DuPage County state's attorney chose to publicly indict him, going as far as asking for the death penalty to punish a man he had ignored as the Nicarico killer for so many years.

Therefore, when Dugan was sentenced to death in 2010, the Coalition publicly opposed his sentence and advocated instead for the elimination of capital punishment due to the way in which the DuPage County criminal justice system had mishandled the Nicarico case and ignored, for more than twenty years, Dugan's admissions to this henious crime. The abolition of the death penalty became law in early 2011. As the governor signed the historic bill, he acknowledged that the mishandling of the Cruz and Hernandez case had been largely responsible for his decision.

In recognition for her efforts, Diana Eiranova-Kyle was appointed to serve as a member of the Illinois Prisoner Review Board but the discovery of an unruptured brain aneurysm that was later successfully repaired prevented her from accepting the appointment.

As for Juan Rivera, (who was mentioned in the Prologue of this book and whose innocence the coalition supported since he was first sentenced to life in prison in 1993) in December, 2011, an appellate court reversed his conviction stating insufficient evidence, and on January 6, 2012, after spending almost twenty years behind bars, he was finally freed. To this day, Holly Staker's killer has not been found and therefore, in her case, justice has not been done.